SILENT POWER

by

Tyesha Roman

Published by
Hasmark Publishing
www.hasmarkpublishing.com

Editor: Judith Scott judith@hasmarkpublishing.com
Cover Designer: Anne Karklins anne@hasmarkpublishing.com
Book Design: Amit Dey amit@hasmarkpublishing.com

ISBN 13: 978-1-77482-003-2
ISBN 10: 177482003X

Dedication

This book is dedicated to the Most High, God, my creator and everlasting provider. Without You, this book wouldn't be possible. Thank You for making room for my gifts and transforming my mind so that I may use it to heal lives all over the world. I am forever grateful for the humbling process You took me through to serve humanity. You get all the glory!

My husband, Anthony, you are a gift from God. Thank you for your patience, love, and support through this journey of self-discovery and living on purpose. I love you, baby!

My children, Aden and Anaya, my angels from above—words can't describe how grateful I am for the wise and free-spirited souls you are. I love you both with everything in me. Thank you for making me a mom. It's the best feeling in the world.

My mom, I love you, and I admire your dedication to supporting my work and my family. You have been such a blessing in our lives. I don't know where I'd be without you. God bless you!

My family and friends, the time has come to learn how powerful you are and live your truth. You can do anything you put your mind and heart into. I believe in you!

Table of Contents

Introduction

Stand in Your Power

I am writing this book about your own personal power to attain freedom, inspiring you to take accountability for your life and change the very thing that matters—your response to the world you live in. In order to be free, you must be willing to break the habit of being yourself and become a witness to the role you play in your own life. No one else is responsible for where you are now and where you want to be.

To create an inner world that changes your outer world demands your energy, focus, and the willpower to change the thoughts that have created your beliefs. This work of stepping outside of yourself and controlling your mind will test your endurance, but you will continue to learn something new about yourself each time you set out to discover your newfound courage to take new action.

You will no longer shrink into the person who is afraid to live boldly and truthfully. Silent power is an undeniable force of strength—*resilience*—that you have within to persist through life's adversity to overcome the pain, judgment, and scarcity that you've experienced. Your resilience picks you back up each time you feel weak, and it drives you to charge at the very things that try to knock you down. No matter how many times adversity strikes or how tired you are, you have the power within yourself to rise above those things to which you have fallen victim to.

Silent Power will help you to witness your life and believe that you are the one who can change it. People don't always believe they're capable of change, and that's the belief that holds them back in the first place. Free yourself from the thoughts that prevent you from accessing the deeper parts of you.

My Story

I am a Latina who grew up in the streets of the South Bronx. As one of four children, I am the only female born to my parents who came to New York from Puerto Rico. At the age of six, I was adopted by my grandmother who stepped up to care for us when Child Protective Services took us away from our parents. Mom and dad were addicted to drugs and had lost control over their lives, as well as ours. I have suffered loss, pain, and confusion about my identity for most of my life. I've held on to guilt and shame because of the things I've been through and where I came from. I blamed everything I had to go through in life on my past, and it was a vicious cycle that I couldn't seem to get a handle on. Being Latina from the Bronx, and having lived in scarcity most of my life, left me feeling unworthy and fearful. I believed I wasn't good enough to live a different life because that just didn't happen for women like me. I got tired of thinking these thoughts and feeling these feelings. Five years ago, I felt the nudge to rediscover my true self, to stand up and fight, to stop blaming others for my circumstances, and take my power back. I lived embarrassed of where I was for far too long, and I knew that no one else was going to come and save me. My life was proof of that.

My innocence, my playfulness, my rest, my security, my stability, and my belief in myself were all taken from me when I felt powerless. I demanded to have them back, and through that pursuit, I have moved many times, left jobs that didn't make me happy, separated from relationships, found myself broke and fearful, all while crying out to try to find what inside of me wasn't allowing me to change. The most difficult times have revealed very powerful lessons, all leading back to me. Fighting to feel like the victim while fighting to take responsibility challenged me in ways that made me want to quit, but I was tired of running away, tired of starting over, tired of no one coming to my aid, and tired of no one having the answers. I learned that no one has them, except for the one living within you.

Today, I am happily married and living in upstate New York with my husband, two beautiful children, and our Maltese Skippy. I'm living guilt-free and reveling in the peaceful life I have created for myself. I coach women who struggle with believing in themselves and breaking up with their past life to be the star in their now. I can help because I was this woman. I was afraid and controlled by my environment. I believed success was possible for everyone else but me. I doubted my ability to become an entrepreneur. I too had a poverty mindset, and I too was afraid to take the action necessary to improve my life. I owe the positive changes in my life to the silent power that just wouldn't let me give up until I witnessed what it promised me—a life of complete trust, freedom, and joy.

From starting my life in a toxic childhood, to spending teenage years in jail, to being addicted to alcohol for more than twenty years, to enduring a two-year separation in my relationship, to making the leap to leave my nine-to-five job with two small children in order to follow my purpose in life, all took bravery that I didn't even know I had until I did them. When I made these deci-sions, I was judged and reminded of all the negative outcomes that would arise from changing who I was to who I wanted to become, but my resilience allowed me to break free from an environment that tried to trap me in what was familiar, and that meant missing out on what God had planned for my life.

How This Book Will Help You

Every chapter will introduce you to a power you have within your-self and help you to understand how it can change your life if you tap into it. You don't have to read the chapters in sequence—start with whatever seems most relevant to your life. Your beliefs will change when you realize what it is that you have been giving your power away to, and how you can take the power within and redi-rect it wherever you are craving fulfillment, peace, and joy. Your faith will get you through tough times, and you don't have to depend on any other human being for your faith to increase. It is an inside job. The resources needed to nurture and heal what's hurting are all available to you. You will not only have unshake-able faith in God, but also in your own God-given gifts and beliefs. You will have the courage to make the decisions that you have feared making in the past. Faith and courage have given me the freedom to leave soul-sucking jobs and relationships and to have more time to invest in my healing, my family life, and my purpose here on Earth.

Chapter 1

The Power of Resilience

Whether you turn to the right or to the left, your ears will hear a voice behind you, saying, "This is the way; walk in it."

Isaiah 30:21

Waking Up!

I'm lying in a quiet room in upstate New York, a peaceful place that I call home, which is about an hour and a half from the Bronx where I was born and raised. It's just past 7 a.m., mid-September, and I'm wondering what exactly happened before I fell asleep because I do not remember. But there's something different about me, almost as if I'm caught in between two worlds. I feel regret and shame weighing heavily on me, but at the same time, I feel this freedom that has awakened in me. It's both painful and liberating at the same time. How can I feel both shame and freedom simultaneously? All my life it's been one or the other.

As I sit up in bed feeling alone in my guilt and shame, I turn to my husband and ask him, "What happened last night?" Part of me did not want to hear the answer, the other part knowing that I have to try to make sense of what is happening within me. I want answers for the shame I am feeling. He tells me, "Again, you drank too much. You were drunk!" I have a confused look on my face and a feeling of disbelief because I drank only two glasses of wine last night. I know he is telling the truth because of how I am feeling—like a bad person. It makes me so disappointed in myself because for the first time in a long time I actually cut down from the usual one to two bottles to stick to a two-drink minimum, which, by the way, is not easy for me at all. I have been trying to change for my family to be a better person, but it's not easy. I have been drinking since I was thirteen years old. Now here I am at thirty-seven still trying to get my shit together and make sense of it all.

My husband continues, "You were on the bathroom floor hugging the toilet, throwing up, so unaware and disconnected from reality, while the kids and I watched you worried sick, disappointed, tired of it, and confused, trying to understand why you keep putting yourself and us through this. Why?" At that moment, my heart shatters into pieces. I am so broken inside, and I don't have the answer to why I struggle so badly with alcohol, why it is so hard to quit, and why although my family is hurting, I do nothing about it. I am supposed to love them, protect them, and show them different from what I saw growing up. I am supposed to be different from my parents and the environment I was raised in. The thoughts begin running wild, and the shame begins growing bigger, the tears welling up in my eyes and falling down my face effortlessly.

What do I say to my husband? Responding with "I don't know" is just ridiculous at this point, so I stand quietly. I can't say

I have a problem because, for one, it's obvious, and two, I always say that when I am desperate to justify the stupid things alcohol makes me do. It has become a sad song that you just get tired of listening to. I am so angry with myself that they have to see me this way—powerless and weak, throwing up my guts—all because I want to drink alcohol, all because I can't find another way to deal with my pain and enjoy my life. I am so sick and tired of acting like everything is all good when it's not. I own that denial card and pull it right out my back pocket when it serves me.

I think back on last night. I only had two glasses of wine. How could two glasses turn me into a drunk mess? Have you ever thought you had something under control, only to realize you've messed up—again—and hurt the people you love—again? I have been trying to cut down because completely quitting has never been an option for me. Alcohol has been a part of my life for so long. Brunch with the girls, holidays, birthdays, vacations, and any accomplishment—whether my own or someone else's—always calls for a celebration. If I get a new client, make a sale, build a new friendship, it's time to toast. The taste, the smell, the warmth, the sense of peace and relief I feel when I drink it, everything about that damn red wine makes me want more and more. It makes me feel at ease like nothing else ever has. Nothing feels better than pouring myself a glass and experiencing that feeling of total bliss. I choose it over company and even food.

Keeping a Promise with God's Help

The night that I decided to not make love with my red wine and to depart from it early so that I could be a mom and wife was the night I lost control of my awareness. I couldn't believe how two drinks made me black out and left me with no recollection of all three of my family members standing at the bathroom door watching me being controlled by this evil spirit I now know to be alcohol. A part of me is relieved that I can't remember any details because I couldn't take another memory of the pain my drinking had caused my family. I knew how long and hard it would be to get the picture out of my mind if I clearly remembered that night.

I beat myself up, thinking, "What a great solution, Tye, a two-drink minimum. Way to go! How did that work out? You are not in control, the alcohol is. When are you going to see that? A two-drink minimum is not the answer. I know you're trying to hold on, *but it's time to let go and say goodbye to this chapter of your life.*" It was almost as if someone else was talking to me or putting these thoughts in my mind because I started to agree with this voice and not reach in my back pocket for my denial card. I was sitting there thinking, "Yeah, you're right—I'm tired. I'm really fucking tired. I am a grown woman with children. I feel ashamed, I'm embarrassed, I have been whipped and beaten by this thing, left almost to die in many past events. I have to just stop and admit that a two-drink minimum is not the answer for me."

While I was still trying to have a conversation with my husband, I was having a conversation with this silent voice that no one could hear but me. As I sat up in the bed, the voice was speaking, the thoughts were flowing, but nothing was coming out of my mouth. I felt shame from my addiction but also this deep knowing in my soul that I was never going to have another drink of alcohol in my life. This knowing grew bigger inside of me, and I wanted so badly to tell my husband that I knew for sure this was it. But how could I look over at him and tell him that this was the last day, when I'd said the same thing so many times before? I had been lying for years to myself and him. I couldn't find the words to justify last night, but in that moment, I had to find the courage to tell him again that I quit for good, that he would never have to worry about my addiction again, and from that day forward life was going to be different. I wanted to say yes to him and no to drinking—no to the friends I drank with, and no to the enemy living in my mind and body who knew my weakness and tempted me to self-destruct. Even though I was strong for everyone else, this was a part of my life where I was the weakest.

Finally, the deep desire of being alcohol free! I never knew I desired to be sober, but your inner self knows your truth and what you want and need long before you know it. I had suppressed the truth for years because of my own traumatic life experiences. I looked my husband in the eyes and said, "I am never going to drink again. I want no part of it. I can't tell you what's happening in me, or why I feel this certain, and why I know without a shadow of a doubt that this is true for me, but it is." Whoo, what a relief. I said it! I said it knowing I meant it. I was not going to go back on my word now.

I thought silently, "Ok, Tye, we got past that one. Now keep going. I know you're worried about what he's thinking, but that's none of your business right now. Keep expressing yourself, even if other voices come up and say, 'you're lying,' 'who are you kidding?' 'you've been here before,' 'you can't quit,' 'you are known for your *Wine Wednesdays*.'" (*Wine Wednesdays* was a live Facebook show I was airing every Wednesday to bring women into community and conversation about the tough things no one wants to talk about.)

The enemy made his presence stronger as I was standing up for myself and making a promise to stand in my power. Despite the toxic thoughts, I felt fully guided and supported. I felt as if I were being held, and I had never felt that before. I was convinced something more powerful than I could ever imagine had planted this power in me overnight, because I was one hundred percent sure of what I saying, and I meant it. I was done drinking.

I looked into my husband's eyes, and I could see the pain, the mixed emotions of belief and mistrust. I knew he wanted to believe me. I knew he wanted sobriety for me. I knew he wanted this to be the end of my addiction. But all he could do was sit back and hope for what I said to be true.

No one can do the work for you but you. For the first time, I woke up not even knowing how to start my day. Part of me wanted to stay in bed all day—that conversation with my husband and within me had been exhausting. But that busy voice in my head wouldn't allow me to rest, and I'd never been able to lie in bed being unproductive. (I'm still working on giving myself the grace to take it easy. Growing up, I didn't view my family as go-getters. As a reaction to this, I've always felt the need to be constantly doing or reading—not lying in bed.)

I sat on the bed and knew that something was different in me, but my husband and children couldn't be so sure of that. I know I just told him I quit, but now I wanted to prove it. How could I when I had twenty-four hours until tomorrow? I felt so much pressure waiting for the day to end so that I could say, "Look, day one in the books for this momma." I also wanted some type of explanation as to where the certainty, the definite decision to quit, was coming from. For the first time, I wasn't questioning myself about whether or not I was lying to my family or me. I knew this was my truth, and it scared me.

My husband said something else happened that night. "You were talking in your sleep but in a different language, in tongues, I thought. I don't know, but it's almost as if you were in conversation with someone. It was a language I never heard before. You were talking to someone, and you kept getting up from the bed and getting back on it. It was creepy. I was freaked out. I was afraid to sleep next to you. I even thought about sleeping on the couch, but I was afraid to leave you alone because I didn't know what was happening to you or what would've happened if I had left you in the room alone."

"Wow!" is all I could say. I couldn't believe what I was hearing. I knew something was different in me—but damn! I was speaking in a different language to someone? What language? Whom was I speaking with? Why was my body getting off of the bed and back on? What was happening to me last night? And how could I not remember any of this? I wondered if God visited me and fought this battle for me. Was my spirit at war last night? Did He save my soul because He saw it was time? Was it going to get worse if last night wasn't my last night drinking?

I have a Bible that a very good friend had gifted me, and she even engraved my name on it. Thank God for her. Even though I had never opened the Bible until now, I knew no other way to find answers to the questions I had for myself. That silent voice was leading me to my attic, and off I went looking in my bin of books. It took me straight to the Bible. Oh Lord, this was going to be so awkward because my husband had never seen me reading this. Why this? Why do I have to open this up, and I don't even know how to read it, what to look for? I was so uncomfortable not knowing what I was doing that I almost wanted to hide it, but I didn't. I opened it. As I flipped the pages, my eyes landed on a scripture. "Your own ears will hear him. Right behind you a voice will say, 'This is the way you should go, whether to the right or to the left.'" (Isaiah 30:21) This started getting creepy for me. I wasn't a believer, I wouldn't say the name Jesus, and I had this whole story that the Bible was a book written and edited a million times by different men. I closed it and sat with that scripture silently. I didn't share it with anyone because I was confused and uncertain. I didn't remember getting up and off the bed repeatedly and speaking as if I were possessed. Now I was dusting off a Bible I hadn't read in years.

I gave my husband a kiss and a big hug and assured him that he would never have to worry about me drinking again. I knew in my heart it was true because I felt a peace that I couldn't understand or explain. I couldn't wait for a month to go by already so I could prove myself to him and the kids. I wanted them to believe me, to be proud of me, to trust me, and to never hurt again because they didn't deserve that. My husband looked over at me and said, "I told the kids last night to take a good look at you and never in their lives touch alcohol." That is exactly what I wanted too. However, knowing that I was the one to be their reason and example made me feel like such a failure. I can't believe how openly I lived this way as if it were normal. Going to get-togethers and celebrations with tons of alcohol everywhere and me always helping myself to it—that was done. It was not cool that my kids had to see me transform and give in to liquid in a cup.

Living Sober

God gave me the power to be resilient and overcome my addiction. Whatever happened that night, I thank Him for it because, as I write this book, I am three years sober. Whatever visited me that night wiped the craving, taste, and need for alcohol from me for good. It helped me fight a battle of detoxing that no one had ever seen. A silent and omnipresent power had answered my heart's deepest desires. God knew I wanted to break free from addiction, but I couldn't do it by myself. I needed His power, a power that flowed to and through me.

Sobriety opened up a new life for me, one I had never known. If you are feeling regret, shame, guilt, and loneliness, and can't bounce back, ask yourself what is taking up your mental space and heart's energy. Sometimes we don't want to admit we need help or to give up the thing that's hurting us because we don't want to believe it's that attachment that's actually hurting us and our families. Sometimes those things seem to protect us, but they don't. Only the power within you protects you. Going within is the key to all of life's wonderful dreams, hopes, and desires.

Chapter 2

The Power of Desire

Know what you want and have the willpower to stand by it. Your mind is all it takes.

What Do You Want?

There comes a time in our lives when we must face ourselves and ask what we want—a time when we look around and realize there's so much more to life than what we are currently experiencing. It's human nature to grow, expand, and progress—and all this happens when you have a desire. This need to grow is why you feel trapped when you settle or when you shortchange yourself. When you do just enough to get by, it will never feel like enough.

There is a supernatural power that delivers more than enough, and that may be hard for some people to believe. Those that do believe still struggle with allowing this power to work in their lives. They can't receive all that God has for them because they feel that wanting more comes with a punishment. But that's not true. *Desiring more comes with a price, not a punishment*—the price you pay will be to give up your old life, the unwanted parts, and go for what you want, trusting that you will have it. You have to let go and surrender to receive the everlasting riches of God. Did I mention you have to be brave? Not smart, not qualified, not in the best position in life—just brave.

To help yourself discover what you truly desire, ask yourself

- Who are you?
- What do you want?
- What gifts do you have?
- What were you called to do?
- What do you need right now?
- What does your heart long for more than anything?
- What areas of your life need a restart? Is it your health, your finances, your relationships?
- What would you love to be doing now?
- What would make you feel relieved right now?

Watch and listen to yourself, pay attention to how you feel, and take a good look in the mirror every day. Your questions are not going to be answered overnight. You just have to show up every day eager to observe and understand yourself at a deeper level. Don't focus on the time it's going to take, but rather on the growth and changes that will happen inside of you. The time will pass anyway.

To Find Answers, Open Your Mind

To understand what you want, it is helpful to change your perspective and receive new ideas, thoughts, and suggestions that will empower you. The biggest mistake I ever made going into anything new, whether it was a book, a course, or an event was to think, "I know or heard this already." I quickly had to learn how to approach life differently, in an open-minded and non-judgmental way, allowing a new world of possibilities to open up for me. I share this advice with you because it works: Be a student in life, just as much as you are the teacher. It will feel uncomfortable going within and answering questions with a new perspective. Who wants to be uncomfortable? I'll tell you who … *You*! It's the reason you are here.

Set an intention and commit to it: "I intend to discover what I want for myself by opening my mind and heart to the truth without judging the things that keep me up at night. I am ready to live a new life." I want you to love yourself and know that your dreams matter. You matter. Your intention is key.

Don't Base Your Wants on Outside Validation

When I was unaware of my truth, I turned to others for validation because I didn't know any better, and that hurt me. No one had what I was searching for, but I kept searching because I knew that if I stopped, I would never know why I was here or what was my purpose in life. Now, I know that whatever it is that you are searching for is already within you, and no one can ever take that away. You are so powerful. I wish I had known this about myself because I would have made better decisions and not buried myself in the holes I'd dug in my search for the truth.

The more you seek outside validation, the further you will stray from your truth. Right now, are you living and building someone else's dreams and not your own? Do you feel as if it's easier to work for someone else than explore your own life's work? I remember feeling the pressure of meeting expectations that were not my own, giving all of myself to make life better for others. That's what work felt like for me, no matter the job I worked.

When you start examining your environment, you see clearly who you're listening to and taking advice from, and what they're telling you your life should look like. I know so many people living in debt, bondage, fear, regret, and pain because of pressure to do things they actually don't want to do. Do you feel pressure when you think about what you want your life to stand for? Success is what *you* want it to be. If you and society have different perceptions of achievement, it's time you owned yours.

I have spent years trying to figure out how to be a better woman, mother, friend, entrepreneur, you name it, but in my heart, my efforts were never good enough. I was never satisfied. Why? Because others weren't satisfied, and I held onto to those memories of disapproval when I didn't do it the way someone wanted me to. I had no idea that in my mind I had the belief *"I am not enough"* running on repeat. Do you know what belief is running on repeat in your mind? Have you ever sat silently to listen to what's going on in your mind? When you discover the thought that's on repeat in your mind, you will understand how beliefs either limit you or cause you to progress. On this journey to finding myself, I funded a lot of other people's dreams and egos because it was easier for me to see the vision for somebody else, but not for me. I was giving my power and energy away every time I believed the impossible to be possible for someone else besides myself, and it's why I hurt myself along the way. We are adept at constantly encouraging, pouring out, and believing in everyone else except for ourselves. Some of us are still waiting to be appreciated and to receive recognition and some kind of reward for the amount of support we give to others. Recognize you, reward you, and support you. You can get lost in this world and feel undeserving if you keep raising everyone else's deserving level and not your own.

So if you have been living for others, letting them determine what you should want, justifying where you are, or thinking it's over or too late, it's time to stand in your power and get focused on the thoughts inside in *your* head because those are the only thoughts that matter.

Why Do We Turn to Others for Validation?

Why is it that we have been so focused on what everyone else thinks about us? Why do we need others to approve of our decisions of who we become and how we live our lives? That's what I wanted to get to the bottom of. I remember one morning sitting on my deck watching the sunlight cut through the clouds, and tears began falling down my face as I held on to my cup of coffee, feeling like the questions in my mind had just been answered: *Tye, you have been stressing yourself out worried about what your mother, brother, and everyone else thinks about you because you value their thoughts more than you do your own.* I had a conversation with God as if He were on the deck with me. He read my thoughts and knew what was weighing me down—the pressure of having to please everyone. I had been asking for a long time why I couldn't move this dark cloud from over me. That cloud was a combination of past thoughts that were controlling my every decision in life, often unconsciously. It was time to break free and be my own woman, free from judgment, fear, pain, procrastination, worry, and self-condemnation. I drank that coffee like a boss and smiled up at the sky.

I realized that for years I made decisions with a preprogrammed mindset. I had been programmed to worry about how my decisions would cause others to react. What a morning of freedom that was! I looked up at the sky once again and knew that something greater than me was giving me the courage to not only think these thoughts, but to act on them.

You might be thinking about what steps you can take to break free of your habitual thinking, and as you can see, sitting in silence and engaging in my mental conversation were my steps. Don't avoid time alone when you have it. Sit in silence and experience the magic.

In the silence, I reflected on another question: *Why are you doing things you don't want to do?* The answer was, "I don't know." In truth, we all know; we're just afraid to call the shots that can change our lives forever. But your environment, the voices in your head, and society are not afraid to call shots—ones that blind you into believing in a success that doesn't work for you or bring God glory. The question then began to change to this one: *What would I love?* Not what would my mother or anyone else want, what would Tye love? Man, I hadn't felt so much liberation in years. Whenever I thought about what I would love, the questions that followed were always: What would others have to say about this? Why do I need their support and approval so badly to pursue the dreams that God placed in my heart? I realized if I kept worrying about everybody else's feelings, I would feel stuck forever, and I was tired of living that way.

Think about all the things you want. Would it be like to start that business, travel the world, spend more time with your family, make more money, be in the best shape of your life, serve more people, and wake up when you feel like it having complete freedom to live life on your own terms? Wouldn't the thought of nothing standing in your way be amazing? You should never stop thinking about your desires. The sacrifices you make should serve you and God, not *man*. Why have we neglected ourselves?

I know someone who dropped out of high school so her partner could continue while she stayed home with the baby. Can you believe he never graduated? Why the heck did she drop out? Because she would have felt guilty had she chosen herself over him. We sacrifice so much for others, and there's a reason for that. Very often, it's not because we have big ol' hearts, it's because we feel *guilty*. Guilt is a weapon of the enemy, and your guilt will rob you, hurt you, and leave you out in the cold. Thoughts of our own desires that bring pleasure and freedom almost seem selfish. Why have the insecurities and fears of others become our own? Why have we procrastinated on our dreams but make it so damn easy for the ones we love to have what they want handed to them? I know you want what's best for the people in your life, but what about that beautiful soul of yours whose desires have not been met? I am a mother and trust me, I had to learn to take care of myself—to eat a whole meal, comb my hair—after I realized loving the people in my life does not mean taking care of myself last.

We are in control of our lives; no one else is. If we don't stop ourselves from catering to everyone, who will? Feeling pressured and limited in what we can do for ourselves is not God's plan for us. You can't feel guilty anymore about taking your time and energy back to become all that you were born to be. I bet if you did things your way and not everyone else's, you would amaze yourself. You can't worry about upsetting people or stepping on their toes anymore. It's time to grow spiritually, emotionally, and financially.

If you're serious about building your dream life, you are going to face a lot of opposition, but you were built for this shit. We have to do the uncomfortable things now, and that includes speaking your mind, making your own decisions, and following through with or without support. Learn to say no to people. It's ok to say,

"I have some quality time scheduled for myself." You don't have to justify your decisions or make them pleasing to others. Get your time back and use it wisely. You can't get yesterday back, so use today to awaken and rebuild yourself.

In order to live free from fear, pain, guilt, shame, and doubt, we must find ways to help ourselves so that we don't count on the external, such as other people, but rather, look within ourselves for the changes we want to see. Start where you are with what you have. It takes a lot of courage and mental strength to evolve while still in the same environment that's draining you and bringing you down, but it's possible. Yes, that means changing without trying to change other people. Changing other people is not your job. It's time to stop the excuses about your spouse or your boss being the reason you are in the position you are in. You have to do the spiritual work so you can feel closer to yourself than anyone else, so you can hear what you are saying to yourself every day.

Be Careful with Whom You Express Your Wants

Be very careful with whom you express the desires of your life. Good and evil exist in this world. Your job is to learn how to discern them, so you don't imprison yourself. You have infinite potential locked up inside of you, and every time you express it, it can either be encouraged or discouraged by others. When it's discouraged, it stays locked inside of you because of your fear of failing and disappointing. Do you ever feel as if your growth is not encouraged for reasons you don't understand? Do you wonder why your support hasn't been out of this world?

People will take advantage of your insecurities and lack of knowledge. Some need you right where you are right now and will not tell you the truth because they gain from you not knowing it. That person could be a spouse, an employer, a co-worker, a friend, or anyone who gains from your lack of wisdom and power. Think about everybody in your environment. Who do you need to spend less time with? Who is always discouraging you and never giving you the credit that is due? Who do you need more time with? Who appreciates the value you bring to their lives? What are the conversations that empower you? Are you having enough of those? How much value are you getting from the relationships you sacrifice your dreams for? Because it really matters.

Learn to guard your mind, and love some people from afar so you can dump all the trash you picked up from them. How many times have you had a great day or a brilliant idea and someone ruined both of them for you with their skepticism? You probably never followed through with the idea and ended up not having a good day. Someone else's mind influenced yours—a mind that has its own thoughts and beliefs. Even those who love you can kill your dreams and ideas if you share them, so you have to learn how to keep some things to yourself. For example, I would tell my husband every crazy idea that ran through my mind, and I had to learn to control that because I am a dreamer, and he is a realist. My ideas weren't always backed by solid plans and measures, so I was just proving to him that he needed to save me from myself. Realists need facts and plans, and dreamers let their imaginations run wild and believe that the plan which they are awaiting will come to them.

So if you're a dreamer like myself, I encourage you to be still and get silent until you feel strong enough to share. The more I shared my dreams, the more opposition I faced. I had to get intentional about my conversations and understand that a dreamer can seem like a threat. I stood away from everybody for a while. I was completely silent, no social media, tv, calls, texts. It may have seemed rude at the time, but I was serious about spending time alone with my own thoughts. I learned that a lot of the thoughts and beliefs associated with my desires were not my own and existed for the safety of others. Beliefs such as, "You can't just quit your job; it'll take too long to build a business. You're too old to start from scratch." Man, who's thoughts were these ... because they weren't mine?

Learn to support yourself in ways that protect your peace. It's a serious commitment, but you shouldn't have to worry because it's nothing you can't handle. If you want peace, there are some things you can't force others to believe, to care about, or to support. They have the right to have their own opinions and feelings. They may be experiencing fears, self-doubt, and worry in their own lives, and you could be compromising yourself if you accept their ideas and let them become your reality. You harm your mind when you leave it open to someone else's doubts and fears, and we all have them.

In no way am I saying your loved ones are responsible for hindering you. I am saying you are allowing them to because you don't understand that they are dealing with their own shit like every human being is. You want support, understanding, and applause, but it takes great work for someone to accept you fully.

If you're comfortable with doing this right now, shake yourself up and get ready to detox some people from your life. Get rid of the heavy people and things weighing you down. Start now with the first person who comes to mind, no matter who it is.

Act Now, and Don't Quit

Once you've decided what you really want, you have to live your life in pursuit of it. There is no such thing as too old, too late, too far, too much. God is unlimited. What do you want more of—money? Great, stop spending the money that you have foolishly and manage it better. Want better health? Great, change the poor health habits of drinking, smoking, eating junk food and lying around all day, and try taking a walk instead. I think that's a great start. My message is to get moving. You need a strong desire, a definite purpose, and the courage to stand by it until it becomes a reality. It's ok to be obsessed with your dreams, and you need nothing to start dreaming right where you are.

Act on pursuing your desires now. It doesn't cost you any money to take action right now, does it? What you do today matters. We have a habit of saying we'll do it tomorrow, not realizing that when we make decisions from lazy and unmotivated states, we work against ourselves. We don't show up for our blessings because we decide to be lazy. Every day, we should be motivated to learn more, do more, serve more, and enjoy the journey. Sometimes the delay comes from fear—fear of starting over, relocating, taking pay cuts, re-inventing yourself, letting go of past relationships, starting a business, or putting yourself first. But how many more years will you let pass by before overcoming your fears so you can have what your heart desires? It's challenging to get in touch with those deeper parts of yourself, especially when you see that they've been you standing in your way all along. We just have to own them and move on.

Your opportunity comes disguised, and sometimes we mistake it for defeat and misfortune. It looks like a hot mess before it gets good. This is why so many fail to recognize their opportunity. They run from the mess. They don't sit in discomfort and get through it. I ran from quitting alcohol for years. It was uncomfortable to quit for many reasons. The enemy said I couldn't, it was too hard, and I was worried about what my life would be like without it.

As you discover and connect with your deepest desires, prepare for adversity. Don't quit when times get tough and things don't work out in your favor. Hold on and keep dreaming big. One of the most common causes of failure is quitting. Love yourself enough to not quit this time. Stop quitting on yourself when you're confused or don't know the *how*. Those are not reasons to quit—they're excuses. Your thoughts are the only things convincing you that you're meant to live in poverty, not in abundance.

Chapter 3

The Power of Faith

Your faith will make you whole.

The hardest thing to do when everything is crumbling around you and within you is to believe that things are going to get better, to believe that God is for you and not against you. You don't want to do the work at that moment to have faith that things are working out for the good. It's easier for you to cry, ask God *"why me?"* and throw your hands in the air, giving up all hope. But that does nothing for your situation. You don't want to sit still, call out to God, and actually wait on Him to work His power in your mind and into your spirit because it's easier to simply complain and expect the worst. It's easier to pick up the phone and call on everybody else with your drama before you call on God. How many times have you run to your partner, a friend, the phone, or social media before you called on God? Your answers to the questions that keep you up at night are not in your homegirl's back pocket, not on your husband's to-do list, and are not your children's responsibility. Stop leaning on others and start leaning on God. When you put the world first and go seeking comfort and answers there, you're left to fight for yourself. No one can give you the power you need to fight your battles. No one can step in for you and touch lives to make a situation turn around for you.

Activate your faith. How do you do that? Unfortunately, we often forget that there is no single formula or "right way" to do anything. Every single formula for how to do or be something is only one person's version of how to do or be that thing. There's always more than one way. I kept hearing that I should remain in faith and continue praying. But before I opened the Bible, I didn't know how to do that. I would seem ok, but secretly be crying inside. (No matter how much we look like we have our shit together, no one has their shit together.) Your way of activating your faith might be different from mine, and I encourage you to follow your own path, even when it looks different and others keep reminding you of who you used to be. Allow yourself to be like a kid again—curious, open-minded, and expecting. The time you spend trying to justify why you haven't gotten it together, you should be using to actually get it together. Start equipping yourself and bossing up your spirit. You may need to accept some invitations you've been declining. Messages could be waiting for you in places you didn't think you belonged or would ever see yourself in. Give yourself a chance to connect, and I'm telling you the voice will speak! I was excited when I started to ask questions, and even more excited when I started to receive answers.

Read the Word

Some of us have had miracles in twenty-four hours. How do you think that happens? With faith, belief in His Word. As a woman of faith, I had to learn to stop running to the world when circumstances were too difficult for me to handle, and learn to run to His Word instead. I had to start opening up the Bible because reading it and praying without ceasing gave me *power*. Some people believe the Bible is just a book with a bunch of stories that don't relate to what we are going through nowadays, but I find it to be a book that shows me how to live. For example, the ten commandments have given me insight on how to live with morals, values, and integrity.

Did I know what I was looking for when I started reading the Bible? No, I didn't. But I was convinced that if I kept opening it up, I would get what I needed. The book that turned my life around and increased my faith was the book of John. The more I read, the hungrier I became for the Word. It was almost as if God were placing me in tough circumstances to see if I would use what I learned. There were times I wanted to react in my flesh and give people a piece of me. That's the nice way to say it now. But I didn't. My self-control was getting stronger as I continued to read the Bible. I was learning what it meant to see through the eyes of God—with pure love, patience, kindness, forgiveness, and I was amazed at how beautiful that was. What would life be like if I could be that way no matter what circumstance I found myself in?

Every time I flipped to a page, I tried to make sense of it. I tried to find meaning from it in my own life. I would meditate on the scriptures, think about what was going on in my life at those moments, hit my coach up for interpretation, go to Google, YouTube, or journal. I was hungry, I tell you. I wanted to know and feel this faith that I had heard so much about. I wanted to believe, surrender, and trust. I felt like a kid all over again, excited that I had tapped into a new part of my life. I started with reading a few scriptures and witnessing my life, but this didn't end after a week, or two, or three. I realized I was studying. I was actually studying the Word, showing up to online Bible study, and scaling up so much knowledge. I realized that studying the Bible wasn't a quick fix for just one situation in my life. I was obsessed. This book wasn't just for a morning and evening read. This was for access to the mind of Christ. This was for wisdom. This was for deliverance. This was a weapon for me and a book of instructions on how to live my life. These principles were for life, health, marriage, motherhood, all relationships, business, and having a growth mindset. When you feel weak or discouraged, lacking the faith to push forward, you study with hunger, with purpose, with intention. And that's what I found myself doing.

Let Your Life Demonstrate Your Faith

My husband and I share different beliefs, and that's fine. I have learned to respect and love him just as I want his respect and love in return. So, if you're on this spiritual journey of seeking God and your partner is not on the journey with you, that's ok. There's no need for you to vomit the Word all over them, drag them to church, or force them to feel what they are not ready to feel. You wouldn't want anyone doing that to you with their beliefs, so be kind and show your partner, friends, and family love and respect. Too many times we push people away when in our hearts we want to help them. I made that mistake, and it's why I'm sharing this with you. Let your life demonstrate your faith, and those you wish to help may allow and receive it if that's God's plan for their lives.

I realized that a whole year had gone by and I had read only two books: the Bible and *Think and Grow Rich*. I wanted nothing to do with anything else. This was God's plan for my life. Because of where I come from, what I've been through, the beliefs I had, and the sins I've committed, I could never see myself being a believer, let alone a Bible reader. But when God has a plan for your life, you see and feel His guidance manifesting in your life. It's silent, but it moves you and directs you to places and things you have no clue what the connection is to your life or problems. I pray for others and for myself so that I can be a blessing to those who don't yet have a relationship with God, that they may witness the transformation in my life and know that I did it all by faith.

Pray to Change *Yourself*

For a long time, one of my deepest desires was that my husband and son would have a wonderful, healthy, and happy relationship. He was always a good dad, but good wasn't good enough. I wanted him to be a mom-dad. We mothers always want our husbands to be as nurturing, affectionate, and attentive as we are. I wanted him to acknowledge every accomplishment, play with the children more, and ask them how they were doing every five minutes to the extent that I was making him feel like a bad father, and it put a strain on our relationship. I just needed the Lord to fix *him*! But that wasn't the answer. God led me to scriptures that I had to sit with. I had to let God deliver the message without me trying to find my own way to satisfy my selfish needs.

As a wife, are there things you wish your husband would do more of and things you want him to do less of? There's nothing wrong with asking God to soften his heart and give him eyes to see your needs, but I encourage you to seek God and start working on *you* first. Admit your flaws and change yourself because when you change, everything around you changes. I was learning to not put my husband down, talk badly about him, blast our business on social media, or call someone up—but to take it to God instead; my true source, the one who will never steer me wrong and never make me look at my husband with negativity or resentment. I made the choice to take to Christ my husband's lack of attentiveness. I did what I thought I was called to do as a wife holding a spiritual position in the home. I chased God with what I thought was righteousness and obedience. I prayed for my husband as if he needed saving.

As time went on, I began to wonder when God was going to work on my husband. I'd been patient, I'd been praying, I'd been filling the gaps for him. I was tired. I wanted him to show up more so I could stop being a helicopter mom. I was working on trusting God and building my faith, and it's why I was studying the Word. I was sure I was doing everything I was supposed to be doing. I was leaving it all at the feet of Jesus, but the same situations were still arising. Why? I love how God tests our faith. I got this download in my spirit: *Pray for yourself.* I answered: "What? Really, God? I have been stressing, being a helicopter mom, chasing the kids down to see if they are ok, making sure they are not hiding feelings of loneliness, unhappiness, or being bullied, and I ask you for help so my husband can be just as attentive, and you say I need to pray for myself. Lord, I don't like this. But, ok, so what am I praying for, God?" *To accept responsibility for the things in my marriage.* I couldn't deny God was talking to me, and I was receiving all this in my spirit. This conviction weighed heavily on my spirit. I felt so guilty, but I didn't yet understand why. I battled with confessing my faults, my negativity in my marriage, and the same stubbornness I blamed my husband of having.

I started to wonder, "What if I began praying for myself and things did begin to change?" That question fascinated me. I was led to realize that for my husband to change, I couldn't just pray and wait on God; I had to change. I thought, "Ok, God, let's do this. I'm going to see if this silent voice is what I think it is— the power to have my spiritual eyes and ears open to hear the needs and desires of my husband so I have to see him the way

God would see him." God showed me in that moment that I had no control over anyone other than myself. I can pray for others, but my prayers don't change them. Rather, it's my own changed behavior will have that impact. When my husband is stressed from work or has heavy things on his mind, I don't want to think he's just being cranky, and I should stay clear. I want to be able to look deeper than the surface. I hope to use spiritual discernment in this area. I hope to be the wife who can meet him where he is and understand that he too needs that love and affection I'm so desperately pressing him to show others.

Sometimes it is best to leave our spouse alone as they deal with situations. Just be sure to still be *one* with your spouse and give them what they need—grace and open arms. My husband needs me to go up to him and give him a big hug, and that's what I have been doing since. I hug him and tell him what a good man he is. This makes him crack up. His smile brings me so much joy, and I had no idea that he needed me to be that for him—his relief. In these moments I feel proud, honored, and victorious as a wife. I am not looking at the surface of things, I'm not wishing he were different, I'm not resenting him or trying to change him. I am seeking God first about what to do to help my husband.

Marriage isn't easy, but when you trust God and have faith in Him, He will show you how to heal yourself and help the people you love. Complaining never changes anything. It actually makes things worse. I remember being in awe of how changing myself had worked miracles in my marriage. I began to see my husband open up and give more of himself to the kids, and because I prayed for myself, I was able to accept that he is one hell of a father and always was, but he needed to be treated and spoken to differently. Whenever I want to help my husband in any way, I take a good look at myself. If his health worries me, I ask myself whether I am stepping up and demonstrating what good health looks like. Am I working on me so he can have that support he needs? This has taken courage and growth because if you knew me before I accepted God into my life, I wouldn't have accepted that kind of responsibility. But that's what a woman of faith does, and that's what I am now.

One of my biggest flaws was that I talked too much. I complained more than I needed to. I would try to explain myself over and over about decisions I made or things I wanted to do. I would sound like a broken record about how the kids needed more attention, or how my husband wasn't doing enough. I tried to make him feel guilty so many times, but I was the one being convicted and just didn't know how to deal with it. God dropped another truth in my spirit, and it was fire. He said: *I believe you are afraid and worried of what others will think of you.* If I wanted to change things, then I should be positive by creating a peaceful atmosphere instead of an atmosphere of chaos and confusion.

Oh, and that constant need for my husband to be present for the kids … God not only answered that for me, but also showed me why I was so needy. He pointed me back to my childhood. I was in need of love, felt alone, ignored, not worthy, and the fears of my own kids ever feeling that way haunted me. My husband had to remind me that yes, we've made mistakes, but our kids are good, they are loved, we are present always, and they know that. His childhood was different from mine. Since his parents were always around, he couldn't understand why I was pressuring him to be constantly in the kids' faces. I was parenting from my own childhood trauma and fears, and that can put a strain on your marriage, so much so that I have had to pray and work to be here now sharing this with you.

I began to love the changes I was seeing in my marriage, and so back to the Bible for marriage scriptures I went, and I came across Proverbs 31:10–12: "An excellent wife who can find? She is far more precious than jewels. The heart of her husband trusts in her, and he will have no lack of gain. She does him good, and not harm, all the days of her life." We are our husband's crown. Relationships don't always work out, but we have to change and pray for ourselves to be a witness to what is true for us and what is not.

Walking in Our Anointing

When we are walking in our anointing, it means we must be walking in the Spirit, which means we are dwelling in peace, being led by God, and chasing after righteousness. Our husbands and children will become witnesses to who God is in our lives and reap the abundance. For me, walking in my anointing is praying, living on purpose, and loving my family unconditionally. When I'm in the Spirit praying consistently for the body of Christ (which is anything the Lord has placed in my heart) then I am in the presence of God. The overflow of the anointing will inspire and amaze others because of the peace they feel coming from you. Your home will be a home of peace, the atmosphere of your workplace will shift, and you will experience a change in communication and intimacy in your marriage because all things will be set on Christ.

I have so much faith in God because of the works I have seen Him do through me. My marriage rocks now, and I love my husband more than I ever have. One summer we drove five hours away with the kids to visit a park, and to say that we had the best day ever is an understatement. Have you ever felt led to go somewhere and you have no idea why? My husband would have complained about driving five hours to visit a state park, but surprisingly, he agreed, and that just confirmed the nudge I was feeling to go there. Together with my husband and our children, we ended the day playing frisbee in the park. The joy I felt in my soul was bursting out of me. I felt the love of God in me, my husband, and my children. On the ride home, he had such wonderful conversation with them, as he always does now, and I sat in my seat quietly looking up into the sky saying, "Thank you, God. You did it. You did it. I had been waiting for days like this forever, and all I heard back was, *I know what you want.*" When we got home, I turned over to my husband, and my eyes welled up with tears. I said, "Thank you for being you, for today, your love, your playfulness, your humor, your patience, your everything. I am so thankful for you. You are an amazing father!" I cried for about two hours. From 11 p.m. until 1 a.m. I was up thanking God and worshipping Him. He let it be known in my spirit that He is and always will be there, answering my prayers and guiding me on what I need to do to receive His blessings.

Faith with a Purpose

You can't merely have faith. You have to have faith with a purpose, and mine was to heal my family and create a peaceful, positive, and loving home—one where we are all thriving, patient with one another, encouraging one another, setting goals together, and enjoying life. I can't tell you how much we have grown because of my obedience to check myself, even when I was frustrated, losing patience, and some days leaning towards doubt despite displaying strength. If it weren't for the power within me to endure all the tough times and believe God promised us a future of hope and abundance, we wouldn't be happy. We would still be trying to figure out how to overcome the want and pain we felt trying to raise kids while healing ourselves.

Know what your purpose is for your marriage, for your household, and for yourself, and realize that your purpose with faith moves mountains. Faith is the secret. You have to do the work and believe that God is for you, that He hears you, and He knows what you want for your life. He knows what is in the deep of you. No more speaking negatively in your house or over your life. Speak the Word, speak life. Speak it with conviction and power. The words that come out of your mouth have power. What are you constantly saying? Are your words life or death? I walk around my house saying God supplies all my needs; I am healed by His power. God's abundance increases in my life, in my marriage, in my children. I say it loud and proud. That kind of activated faith changes you; it changes the world you see for yourself. Study, pray, and believe with purpose. My life depends on the Word. I love being a woman of faith. I look for purpose in everything I do and in everything I try to overcome.

Faith Is Action

Faith is about belief, and what do we do when we believe? We take action. Faith without works is dead. You can sit there and believe God, but if you are not doing the work, then you won't receive the blessings and changes you are praying for. Do you ever wonder why you keep asking God to help you leave your job and start a business, improve your health or your relationships, or take away your pain, inflammation, sickness, stress, and financial worries, but things are still the same? Faith without action is not going to cut it.

What can you do differently today in your life? What can you do differently in your finances? What can you do differently in your marriage, or in the way you raise your children? You have to settle in your heart and soul that the Word of God is true, and it's not just some words on paper in a book. Act on your belief. When you pray with a purpose for God to work in a particular area in your life, you have to act on that belief. What happens is we don't see what we want to happen right away, so we forget about our purpose, we forget how much we cried and stayed up late at night begging for it. Tired of feeling defeated? Do something. Tired of your financial stress? Stop living above your means. Tired of showing up every day to work? Take action. Ask God to show you what's next for you.

Start praying and spending more time in silence than you spend being distracted. The best guidance is silent—it's powerful and knows the way. You no longer have to be confused when you sit in silence with God. Don't give up because a month goes by without seeing results. Keep trying, keep believing, keep seeking, keep trusting. His Word is powerful. Be full of it, and whatever you ask of Him, He will do it for you. Have faith that something much bigger and more powerful than you knows the way for you. Think about why you need to believe in God, and start praying for Him to soften your heart and heal your wounds. Pray for revelation. God will answer you in your dreams, through other people, through books, or through the Holy Spirit. Start paying attention to the signs, conversations, and happenings that start taking place in your life.

I don't see God as a person, or as someone separate from me. I see God as living in me, a spirit, forever present and expressing itself through me, and as the knowing that I feel when I'm driven to write, speak, coach, and live life on purpose.

Your Power to Forgive

Real healing began when I was able to forgive and look at the people who hurt me, including myself, through the eyes of God.

Right now, there are people all over the world who are lonely, missing somebody, depressed, hurt, scarred from the past, having personal issues no one knows about, or who have secrets you wouldn't believe. They wish, they dream, and they hope. If this is you, I'm writing so you don't feel alone anymore.

I remember feeling alone in a mental prison that I couldn't break out of. I missed what life was like when I loved myself. I missed the woman I used to be—so alive, so free, and unstoppable. I would dance the night away like no one was watching. What happened to me? Why did I begin to hide and become so isolated? What happened to that beautiful soul I used to be? It seemed so long ago that laughter would come from the depth of my belly and penetrate the souls in the room, healing those in need of my infectious joy. When did this shell begin to grow on me?

Sitting on my deck where I spent most of my deep, reflective moments in nature, sipping tea and staring into the sky, I remember thinking I didn't want to be strong anymore; I just wanted to be free in my soul. Strong meant I had too many things to carry, too many battles to fight, too many people to protect—including myself. I'd had enough hiding the pain and picking up the sword. I didn't want to live with my guard up. I was tired of trying to tear down the walls. I didn't want to believe people were out to get me or praying for my downfall, or that I didn't have what it took to make my dreams a reality. I didn't want to believe that where I came from was going to prevent me from where I wanted to go. I'd had enough of these thoughts. I just wanted to live God, to be free to live a new life without secrets and shame within. When people looked in, I wanted them to see pure beauty and truth. I wanted to be a glass house, full of radiance—stones being thrown at it not even being a thought in my mind. I wanted God to show me what life was like without constant war.

My emotions were growing stronger, and tears began to fall. I became silent and asked God to reveal what I needed to do, and He did. Sometimes we sit in our feelings in a chaotic headspace, but not in silence, and don't even give God the time to respond, to show us the way. First Corinthians 2:10 says, "For to us God revealed them through the Spirit: for the Spirit searches all things, even the depths of God."

I heard a voice say, *You have to forgive.* I felt that so deep in my spirit but resisted: "Forgive? Oh man, come on God, I know this sounds simple, but I'm struggling to accept that this is the answer. Forgive whom? Can I just move on not being mean to those who have hurt and offended me and live life? Isn't moving forward and living my life forgiving?" *No, it is not.* This voice was going to be the death of me on that deck, but I felt the need to stay seated and continue this conversation. This was my truth that I had to listen to, and as badly as I wanted to run away and ignore it, I just couldn't. I knew that if I ignored this voice, I was not going to be able to get over feeling weak, lonely, hurt, and scarred from the past and deal with the secrets inside that no one knew about.

How Can I Forgive?

The overwhelm comes on when we don't know how to forgive. That's normal. You're not alone, even if you don't have a relationship with God. God is omnipresent and is just waiting on you to acknowledge Him. If you don't know where to start, you are not alone. If you don't want to forgive, you are not alone. Forgiving is not an easy thing to do. Millions of souls across the world refuse to forgive, and it's why they can't seem to move forward or simply believe in themselves. There's so much judgment held within them, and they don't understand how toxic it is to their life. They can fake their entire life on the outside if they choose to, but they can't ever lie to themselves. They will feel the dissonance within that hinders true integrity. No one can live freely that way, and they know they're not free but are avoiding the very thing necessary to live a life of wholeness.

When was the last time you sat in silence in search of your truth and were honest with yourself about how you really felt and what you'd been avoiding? What is the truth about you? I believe much of what we share about ourselves is not who we really are. We give only enough from the surface because the deep is personal, it's dark, and, well, it's nobody's business. We won't share our real thoughts, emotions, and desires because it hurts to even think we own them. Someone made us feel wrong when we did share them, and we've been wronging ourselves ever since. We are afraid to learn what is going on inside of us and the steps we have to take to experience the freedom we crave.

Some of us, myself included, have been through trauma and pain that have shaped who we are today. If you recognize yourself here, I'm writing this especially for you. Many of us hold on to old memories of when someone made us feel unworthy. We internalized those feelings and began to feel unworthy about everything. We may have been rejected as young children wanting to sing, laugh out loud, dance, run, play, be adventurous and expressive, but we were told to cut it out, sit down, be quiet, relax, aim lower. And if no one never said those things to you or around you, they might have demonstrated them with the way they lived their lives and encouraged you to live yours.

Some of us were violated and disrespected, made to feel unimportant. Some of us were black sheep, constantly being held responsible for others and yelled at when we were just trying to be kids and enjoy our lives, crying to be held and loved but never receiving love or affection. We may have had to care for others when we were the ones who needed to be loved and cared for. We witnessed abuse over and over again and felt helpless as it continued. You start to believe you have no control over the things that happen in your life because of a time when you felt helpless, and it's a belief that stays with some people for years, even until the day they die. That could have been me. We feel ashamed about our past, that someone hurt us, left us, disappointed us. We even feel ashamed of the things we've done because of our own personal trauma. That doesn't make you a bad person. You have just made bad choices, and seriously, who hasn't?

Our thoughts, beliefs, and feelings all start at home. From a very young age, we were programmed to feel and live in fear⊠fear of getting your ass kicked, not doing things right, mom or dad having a bad day and taking it out on you, not being able to fix the problems around you, and on and on. My home certainly had its issues. However, we are not here to blame our parents but simply to peel back the layers from our past that may have a hold on us today. We're here for awareness and freedom, to free our souls from the darkness that we had to endure as children.

I feel you and I see you. I honor you for being so brave and enduring your painful times, but I don't want you to be in pain any longer. I don't want you to live in fear when it comes to shining your light and sharing your heart with the world. My heart goes out to you, along with my six-year-old self, and I want you to know that you are loved and needed. That child still lives in you and wants to be your best friend and do things together, laugh, enjoy life, and create the best of memories. You have to go back and look at the child you were, smile, and say thank you. It's because of that strong child that you are here today. You have fought so hard to stand in your power and stay alive. Be proud of yourself. You probably fought your battles and those of your sisters and brothers too.

We are adults trying to get it together and raise a beautiful family or empower a community to be strong like we are. We are born to express our love, yet because we're withholding it along with our gifts, desires, ideas, and even our whole selves, we break down when we can no longer take the pain. We become a burden we were never meant to be to our husbands, friends, families, and even our kids.

Can you see how the cycle repeats? You had to deal with the bullshit of your parents, caregivers, adult figures. And if you don't heal, guess who has to deal with your bullshit? The people closest to you do. You can see why I have committed to forgiveness and healing. I don't want my kids to feel the absence of love and worthiness like I did. I don't want them to experience fear when I'm working through my own trauma and emotional blocks. So when you think you have to love your kids, you'd better believe that you have to love yourself too.

Forgive Yourself First

We grow old suppressing our past pain, and it doesn't allow us to express our deepest desires; pain is sitting right on top of them pushing them further down. We hold on to so much in fear of letting our past mistakes come out of the closet. You have to learn how to forgive yourself first. You have to create space in your body for new love and energy to make their way through. You've got to clean house, and throw out all the things you think you're wrong for.

I get it, others haven't forgiven you, so you shouldn't forgive yourself. Some people may never forgive you, but you don't need their forgiveness. You need yours. You can't keep punishing yourself for the mistakes you've made in the past or keep holding on to the old memories and using them to justify your present life and actions. If you can't forgive yourself, then who will? You need you. You owe you an apology, a huge kiss, a bubble bath, a hug, a walk, a means to prove that you do love you.

I'll tell you why I had a hard time forgiving myself for the stupid shit I've done in the past and the things I've put up with knowing I shouldn't have. I had this identity of being strong and hard on myself because of the way life felt—hard on me—and I stood with that attitude that honestly did not serve me. I beat myself up more than anyone else ever has. We blame others for our pain, but who's the one reminding us of our past mistakes? We are. Yeah, you have some family that loves reminding you of the shit you've done too, but that's why you have to forgive them too. It's ignorant and indicative of low-vibrational energy to talk about yesterday every day. Who does that? People who live in the past. We don't want to live our past; we want to close the door to it, heal, and start anew, as we are given the grace to do every morning. We have to be more compassionate with ourselves. I'm struggling with this because compassion, to me, meant soft and caring—traits I wasn't much used to. Clearly, I felt my own parents didn't care about me, so why would anyone else?

My father is no longer here with me, God bless his soul, but I learned so much after he passed. I was eventually able to see him for the beautiful soul he was and not the man who hit my mom or battled with drugs; a loving human being who wasn't loved and cared for the way he deserved to have been. He truly was an angel and the kindest man ever in his later years, even when he had done so much to hurt others. He showed me that he forgave himself, and even though he struggled, he wasn't going to live the rest of his life punishing himself for the mistakes he made. That's powerful because the world around him, including myself at times, made him feel that his ability to live without regret was somehow a smack in the face to those he hurt. I was so wrong to even think that way. His ability to not live in regret and not worry about what others thought about him took guts and fearlessness. He showed me how beautiful forgiveness was for oneself.

Believe me, forgiving yourself is the best gift you could ever give yourself. Forgive yourself for telling the same story; it's time for a new one. Forgive yourself for the times when you didn't go for it. Forgive yourself for blaming others when the choice was all yours. Forgive yourself for believing that someone else had the power to decide what was best for you. Forgive yourself for not telling your story when someone else needed to hear it. Forgive yourself for the mistakes you've made. Let them go. Forgive yourself for treating others unfairly. Forgive yourself for not trusting your own instinct. Forgive yourself for putting you last. Forgive yourself for the anxiety and outbursts you've had. Forgive yourself for the time it's taken you to get it together.

Forgive Others to Heal Yourself

Forgiveness is not sweeping your shit under the rug; it's accepting the things that have happened and the choices you made and making peace with them. Forgiving others is not giving power to the person who hurt you. It's about making peace with the fact that hurt people hurt people. You are only hurting yourself and the people who have to live this life with you if you refuse to love yourself enough to heal.

The first time I tried to forgive, I failed at it. I visited my dad in the hospital and told him, "I forgive you. I love you," and I even cried. I felt some relief that I could bring myself to do that after thirty years of holding a grudge, but my heart still felt so heavy. Forgiveness is deep work. It's the heart's work. It's not an intellectual thing. You can't say you forgive and still harbor feelings of resentment and anger. You can't keep bringing up old shit, and you can't keep blaming the person and throwing forgiveness out the window when they or you mess up again. We will spend the rest of our lives forgiving—forgiving people who stepped on your new shoes, who messed up your order at the drive-through, who gave you the wrong results, who stood you up. Get used to making peace in your life because no one else can do it for you. It's your responsibility.

Forgiving Isn't Easy, But Keep Trying

If you can't forgive someone on the first attempt, don't let the fear of failure prevent you from trying again. We tend to base our present decisions on our past, but I don't want you to carry your past into the present anymore. Repeating the same story year after year is exhausting, and as people grow around you and heal, you are left alone to wallow in your past. Then you'll think people don't care about you or don't understand. Don't leave yourself stuck behind a wall, all alone.

We learned to walk by repeatedly failing to stand up straight and strong. Failure came before accomplishment. Let's make peace with that. We failed a million times putting thread through a needle, making the perfect dish, every time we took action before we could get it right. Why are we afraid of failing now? Because failure was bad in someone else's eyes. We were raised to believe that if we fail, trying again is just a plain ol' stupid, embarrassing waste of time and effort. How could we believe these lies when failure is what drove us to walk, stand up, and feel accomplished? Why do we settle because we're afraid of things not working out on the first try? Please tell me what have you done only once and become a master at? There may be something in your life that you want to do right now but you're afraid it's not going to work out for you. You're afraid of starting over, the challenges you'll have to overcome, or believing failure is some kind of set up for destruction.

I was willing to give forgiving others another shot, even though I failed so miserably at it in the past. I was tired of holding on to everything, tired of my heart feeling heavy, and tired of feeling like a fraud for not doing the things I said I was going to do. It was weighing me down and slowing up my life. I learned that in life you don't just try once, and you fail only when you quit and refuse to try again. So here I was taking myself down memory lane so I could be clear on who I needed to forgive and be intentional about it. Some people believe that revisiting the past will leave them there, but that wasn't the case for me. I knew that my past was not a place to live back then, and it sure isn't a place to live now. I just wanted to make peace with it already so I could move on.

Hurt People Hurt People

Growing up in dysfunction isn't empowering at all. It's painful, and it's traumatizing. For us who've experienced it, dysfunction at an early age exposed us to fear, harm, pain, judgment, and suffering, and has been holding us back from being our authentic selves ever since. I've gone through life spending more time complaining and crying about my problems than searching for solutions, and this is why I've carried the pain for so long. But God knows when our hearts are weary and burdened. It's why I was sitting on the deck searching for Him and asking Him to tell me what I needed to do to drop the hustle, the tough shit, the old stories, and just live in flow. You just get tired of that shit when you see yourself living the same life year after year. I didn't want to be mean, cold, hold grudges, or feel unfulfilled anymore, as if my life was missing something. That energy eats you up alive inside. The first people I had to forgive after myself were my parents.

Growing in the Bronx by Yankee Stadium was my earliest childhood memory. I was six years old. My parents had a beautiful three-bedroom on Woodycrest Avenue. I remember the playground right across the street, the bodega right underneath the building, and the school I attended was within walking distance, only a few blocks away. My parents were always fighting and screaming at each other. It was an unstable environment. My parents were addicted to drugs, and my father used to beat my mother. Those are the things I can remember. I'm sure there had to be great and peaceful days, but we always remember the events that changed us.

I remember mom being so beautiful, working a job but living a double life out in the streets with my dad, probably following him around making sure she had his back. Who knows? I can't even imagine the pain she was hiding and for how long, trapped between trying to be a good mom and dealing with mental, physical, and emotional abuse. My beautiful mother used to be gone for hours, and I had no idea where she was. I yearned for her presence. I missed her, I loved her, I needed her, and I wanted her to be there for me so bad, but I couldn't make her do that. I felt powerless and unworthy that she wouldn't rather be with me than whatever other places she chose to be. I know she needed an escape of her own to deal with the shit she was going through. At least I know that now as a mom myself.

Drugs are powerful. They change people and tore my family apart. I had to witness my mom and my brothers getting their asses kicked. I had to stand there and watch while my heart hurt so bad because there was nothing I could do, yelling and begging my father to stop so mom could breathe, so she could stand up, so she could leave him. But she didn't have the strength to leave him, and looking back now, for any woman to pick up with three young children and leave an abusive man doesn't even seem like an option, especially if this man provides for you financially and happens to be the father of your kids. I never understood why my father beat my mother so much, but it hurt me, and I went to school like that and fell asleep thinking about that. I played outside with friends with my parents on my mind, afraid, wondering when the next outburst was going to be. I almost expected it. I felt so guilty trying to be a kid because I felt like I was supposed to be protecting my mom, standing up for her, and hiding her. Why was I being a child when I was supposed to be fighting with her and for her? I'll never forget the day I tried to stand up to my dad. His expression put the fear of death in me, and he said, "Don't you dare!" with his finger pointed at me. My heart hurt. I had to back away and watch him beat mom until he was done. Life became a blur with no sense of family, love, or respect, and home was never home. I think of my six-year-old self; she and my mom must have been so afraid, so alone, so confused, so hurt, so ashamed that the neighbors knew what was happening. How did mom do it? How did she not commit suicide? How did she not run away? How did she take these beatings and get up the next day to be a mother and to go to work?

Things got really bad, and the furniture, my toys, everything was going for sale and out the door right before my eyes. My grandparents were going to adopt us. I can't tell you the pain six-year-old Tyesha and her brothers felt. They were trying to be strong, but they were hurting too. They couldn't express themselves because they didn't have a right, or an ear that would really listen to them and give them the undivided attention that they needed. No one was going to listen to them. The plan was to make sure we had a safe place to live. I can see how our mental health wasn't addressed, and I don't blame anybody. I honestly don't think Puerto Rican families even believed in therapy. They were too worried about other people knowing our truth. I was also afraid that if I spilled my true feelings, my parents would never get us back. Can you imagine a child holding back secrets because she's afraid of what will happen to the family? How unfair that was for me to have to withhold something so important to protect our family when I was the one who needed protection. To be taken and placed in another unwanted environment was emotionally hard for me. I missed my parents and stayed up at night wondering where they were, what they were doing, and if they were ok. I worried about my mother more than my father. I wished she knew how much I missed her at that time, but I was just a kid, and I never learned how to fully express myself when for years I had to hide things and keep quiet because I was afraid.

Reckoning with a Painful Past

I recently hired a trauma coach to help me visit my six-year-old self and heal my wounds. I cried meeting my childhood self, but I got to hug her and tell her how much I loved her. I thanked her for being so strong and holding on. The tears wouldn't stop pouring down my face. Man, I held on to my parents' mistakes for way too long. I felt guilty for years, and I realized that's when I lost my power and became afraid to use it. My father's words—"Don't you dare!"—stayed with me. Even though I've done some courageous things, as I'm sure you have, I am still afraid to do many other things in life. I held on longer than I should have, but I was hurt and didn't know any better. I didn't know how my past was affecting my life until I realized I couldn't go any further. I couldn't get past a certain level of happiness and success. So when God said I needed to forgive, I knew He wanted me to let go of the resentment that only He knew I was carrying in my heart. He wanted to heal me from the things I couldn't let go of by myself. He's so good like that—so loving, so kind.

Going back to where I experienced hurt and pain early on in my life was healing. Healing is never going to look like what it is because of the work that goes into it, but once it's done, you feel a weight lifted off your shoulders. I'm grateful to have been guided to do it, and I don't regret it at all. We've got to listen to our deeper selves. What about you? What have you been feeling the nudge to do about your own healing and happiness? Are you afraid to do it? Or are you not sure what that looks like for you? Use some silent time to reflect and see what keeps coming up for you, and stop ignoring it. Whatever it is, trust that voice is you talking to you.

We all have healing to do. We have to start where we are now and stop ignoring the wounds because they will not heal themselves. Your unhappiness and unfulfillment will visit you again, and you'll think it's because of something material like needing more money. It's the deep of you needing your acknowledgment and focus. Can you think of something you're holding on to? Something someone said about you, something someone did to you? Sometimes we visit only as far back as the last boyfriend, the last heartbreak, the last job that didn't work out for us, and we can't heal. Those things might just be what's on the surface. We don't go back far enough and deep enough to the start of where we experienced that traumatizing fear, that shame, that guilt that shaped you and stood trapped inside your body.

The guilt of not being able to save my mother, change my parents, save us from drugs and separation stayed in my body. I'm forty years old, and I think of all the mom guilt, wife guilt, just guilt, guilt, guilt, causing me to always put other people's needs before mine. Why do you think that is? I can see where it all came from, and I hope you can too in your life. We have experiences that programmed us that way. We've been programmed from childhood, and if we don't forgive ourselves for sitting in our shit longer than we should have, or forgive our parents for their past, we will never be able to begin the process of reprogramming our minds. I've done programs and repeated affirmations, but the real healing began when I was able to forgive and look at the people who hurt me, including myself, through the eyes of God.

My inability to express myself and be heard affected my adult relationships, and even my relationship with my own children. How can we express anything other than what we lived? How can we learn to talk to our children, be patient with them, not judge them, and see them as the beautiful angels they were born as when we cannot break the habit of being our old selves? How can we express ourselves fully when we were punished for it? How can we express ourselves to our husbands without feeling small and weak? How can we be vulnerable when being vulnerable is what got us hurt? So many worries and concerns are hindering us from starting over. Trust me, healing is a lot of work, but it's an every-day job. It's trial and error. It's trying to express yourself, trying to be vulnerable, and trying to take the risk of being shamed and criticized. But we have to try without worrying about or predict-ing the outcome. We have to try again to free ourselves. No other human being is better than you. When you're worried about what others think of your journey of forgiveness and newfound truth—guess what—they probably haven't even started to get their own shit together. Because a healed person will never have intentions of hurting you, but will instead be there to support you.

I've coached many women, and they feel embarrassed to say, "I am scared that I'll never amount to anything great." Shit, I was afraid to admit such a thing to another woman, but now I know why. My old self and my old story were that you don't share the truth. I'm telling you, when you can be as real as it gets, you expe-rience some serious freedom.

How can we tell our stories as women when we are ashamed of them? It's hard. Some of us were called gossipers, cry-babies, attention seekers, and even "hoes"—a hoe—one who sells her soul. How could we be compared to these women as children because we were looking for love and a shoulder to cry on? We were made out to be people who couldn't handle our problems on our own, but shame on you if you wanted a therapist, right? I'm Latina, and therapy was for "white people." We're living in times where the world is changing, and we need each other more now than ever. Crying in silence is a thing of the past. It never heals those deep wounds that keep you feeling stuck. You don't have to do that anymore. You are not alone.

The Way Forward through Forgiveness

If we want to live our best life, we have to forgive those who made life difficult for us so that we can begin to express ourselves in a way that serves us and attracts the people and things we want in our life. The way we live our lives will always be evidence of whether or not we are truly free. You can't fake this; the pretense will show up in your relationships, the language you use, and your attitude. You have to do the work yourself. You have to be free in your mind and in your heart before you can experience real abundance and freedom. Who do you have to release? Who do you have to stop thinking negative things about? Who do you have to stop having arguments within your mind?

We have to forgive others for their wrongdoing, for their mistakes, for their past. They are human just like you and me. We probably even repeated our parents' mistakes and want our children to forgive us, so how can we not forgive our parents and all the others? We don't know what circumstances led them to live in scarcity, abuse, and pain, and then to pass it on to you. Your parents may have had a rough life too. You don't know the pain they had to suffer. So grow up and be wise enough to not dwell on the things that are going or have gone wrong. When you are dissatisfied with your life, ask yourself, "What am I holding on to? What haven't I gotten over? Who haven't I forgiven?" There are things we are not proud of sharing, but it's these unpleasant experiences that hold us back, and we need to release them. We need to be brave enough to treat people like human beings, even if they haven't been the greatest to us. People don't know what they don't know, and remember, they are always doing the best they know how to. It may not seem the best to you, but you don't know what they're struggling with and holding onto. Be kind no matter what. If you have nothing nice to say, say nothing at all.

If it's been hard to share your story because through life you might have heard, "Don't share that with anyone, that's none of people's business. They are going to say things about you that you won't like. You will be judged," I want you to write a letter to yourself of all the things you want to say and get off of your chest. Then rip up the letter and be done with it. You might find you'll love doing this and adopt a journaling practice. Start somewhere, but let loose those things you hold inside. Also, it's tough for the people who played a role in your life to have to hear about the way you perceive them, and we're not here to hurt anyone. So write and let it out. Talk to God and let it out. If we want to heal, we can't live with the thought that we must protect our feelings. When you reach an awareness that no one has power over your feelings, you'll stop living in such a protective mode. There won't be a need for it.

We are all responsible for how we perceive things and how we feel. You're not a child anymore; you're allowed to speak up and use your voice. You have the power to reject what you don't want any part of in your life versus being hurt by it and holding on to it for dear life, as if you're teaching someone a lesson. Spend time with God, and share your heart with Him first. He will show you how to go about handling the objections and obstacles you will face as you reprogram how you deal with the world outside of you. He will help you be strong when forgiving.

Acknowledge to yourself those people who you feel unforgiving towards. Who are you holding anger toward? Who are you jealous of? Who do you secretly hate? You can't say you forgive them, and say "I hate him," or later say "God forgive me, but never I'll forgive him," without feeling any shame or remorse. I can't even tell you how contradictory that is. You can't conquer or overcome what you don't confront. Be honest about your true feelings, even if your past has made that hard for you. God can't help you heal what you won't admit to and put effort into working on.

Releasing what doesn't serve us requires our willingness to be uncomfortable. For a long time, I wasn't willing, and I know that now because of how much alcohol I drank (my super suppressor). How much I complained and felt the need to talk about the past. How much I blamed others for my circumstances: "If only they could be the way I want them to be, my life would be better. If only they would change who they are, how they live their lives, how they think, all the way down to how they treat me, I would be happy." Do you find yourself trying to change someone or control everything that makes people who they are? You've got to ask yourself why that is. Then you've got to do the work to stop that behavior because it's hurting you and doing nothing great for them. When you let go of what's no longer serving you, you realize the only person who needs to be changed is you. And that's ok. Be willing to change. We all have work to do. It doesn't mean something is wrong with us. We can learn how to accept others for who they are. We can learn how to have compassion for all the things they've been through. We can love again without controlling, judging, blaming, or changing them, and criticizing everything they do. How could that person ever be beautiful in your eyes if you're unwilling to release these behaviors that don't serve you? We can make the relationship beautiful again, but we must start with ourselves first.

We need to feel safe, understood, and loved in order to heal. And that takes time. You are worth the time, no matter what your past looks like. You're allowed to stop carrying it around, justifying it, and thinking of it. It's ok to put it down and be free. Asking for help is ok too. We all know we need it. None of us is going to make it alone. I'm grateful for all the people who have helped and are still helping me to improve my life. God has already blessed you with a friend, mentor, coach, community, or support system. Are you willing to receive the many forms of God's blessings? Are you willing to make space for new things in your life? The hardest part is letting go, but you got this!

Chapter 5

Your Power Over the Enemy

Fear is the gateway to spiritual and financial poverty.

What Was Controlling Me?

When I began to take a deep look at my life, I wasn't fulfilled, and I wondered why was this my life. How was it possible to continue living a life that I hated? I felt like I was making the same mistakes over and over. What was controlling me? Why did I continuously make choices that I would later regret? If you're unaware of what's controlling your life, and you're sick and tired of having to live it every day, have the guts to focus on it. Negative energy equals negative results, and negativity has controlled us for far too long. Why won't it go away? It's present only because we keep it alive. It's not only alive, but also powerful and always flowing to the person who attracts it. Have you've been living an unfulfilled life for years, and despite how hard you've tried, you can't seem to shake the emotions and discouraging feelings you have? They won't allow you to make massive changes in your life, and that keeps you up at night wondering what's wrong with you. You're still searching and trying to climb the wall that you've built and can't see a way over. Close your eyes and imagine the wall. How thick is it? How tall? Does it have holes, or is it solid?

When I first did this exercise of closing my eyes and seeing the wall I built, it was thick, tall, and had no holes. It was solid, and I knew I had work to do. I was committed to healing myself and helping others figure out how to do the same. We all have a past, and some of us are still living there. Let me tell you why you are still waking up and crying about yesterday, living in regret, complaining about your life, and feeling defeated. The devil, that's why. He has made his way in the best way he knows how—through your mind.

You built that wall and isolated yourself, and isolation is the devil's playground. It's easy to attack someone who doesn't easily trust people, who has become skeptical over the years, who gives their time to negative news, videos, friends, and drama. Trust me, you don't have to leave the house for this. So if you're going to say, "Well, I don't hang out with any of my old negative friends," you don't have to. Your mind is a playground, and he lives only in the minds of people who live in fear—fear of being hurt, trusting, changing, or believing in themselves. What are you afraid of right now? What are you struggling with? What changes are you afraid to make? What keeps you up at night? You can no longer ignore what's happening because year after year you live out those hidden feelings, doubts, and fears in your day-to-day life. You know, like when we settle for less than we deserve, and then want to die because of it. We want to start life all over. I can't tell you how many times I wanted a do-over.

Planting Fear

The enemy moves in and occupies the unused space in your mind. He's clever and knows how to plant seeds of fear in your mind to control you. The more they are used, the more those seeds will grow. Ask yourself how often you live afraid—afraid of quitting a job that makes you unhappy, afraid of leaving a relationship that you know is broken and doesn't serve you, starting a business, getting in the best shape of your life, your money not growing, or not giving your kids the life they deserve. We spend our days living in fear, even when we look like we're having fun. What are you really thinking and feeling? Because that's what's real, not what you portray on the outside.

The devil knows what he's doing. He is shrewd, and loves planting fear and watching you shrink and give up on your dreams because you're too afraid to go out there and try, to ask for help, to fail, and to make mistakes. You're too afraid to be seen in your process of transformation and growth, and afraid to admit that you want more because of the shame you will feel for where you are now. He is very clever, and he knows the fears that control most people are those of poverty and death. How many times do you think about being poor, and it scares you? You spend more time thinking about being poor than you do being rich because you've never been rich, and you don't know what that looks like. We have to learn how to see a life for ourselves that we've never lived. That's the beauty of dreaming. When you make space in your mind to dream, you leave less room for the devil's seeds of the fear of poverty. You may have sat with yourself many times wondering when your life was going to be different, when you were going to have all the freedom, peace, love, and abundance that you wanted and so rightfully deserved. Can you see the tight grip he has on you? Those thoughts are planted so deeply within you that you believe them to be yours. I'm here to remind you of what the Word of God says in 2 Timothy 1:7: "For God hath not given us the spirit of fear; but of power, and of love, and of a sound mind." The enemy has a grip on all people who allow fear to paralyze them.

Choose the Light

While fear is natural—and yes, we *all* feel it—those who are bound by the enemy allow fear to control them. Those who believe in the light of God trust that they can do anything, and it will all work out for their good, no matter the time it takes. God loves you, and he wants you to walk in your purpose. He wants you to develop a relationship with Him so that you no longer believe the lies of the enemy. The devil can't punish anyone, except in that person's own mind. Most of the things we fear don't even exist. Who says you can't build a successful life for yourself? Who says if you quit that job that you'll never find your calling and true happiness? Who says you don't have what it takes and that you're not enough? The enemy, that's who.

It's not God, and that's for sure. God is light and love and wants you to live in prosperity all of your days. Why? Because that brings Him Glory. How can we glorify Him if we are living in fear and constantly making excuses about why things won't work out for us? We won't even know that unless we take the leap. You believe things won't work out because the thought is so deeply ingrained in your mind.

You're probably wondering how you can get the enemy out of your mind and begin to trust God, knowing that you're chosen and deserving. You have to start thinking differently. That's right, you have to use your mind in a way that you haven't used it in a long time. Use it constructively in a way that serves you and gives you feelings of hope and not fear. There's a Zig Ziglar quote that my husband put on the fridge for all of us to see every day: "Positive thinking will let you do everything better than negative thinking will." It's such a good reminder. I am a fan of quotes around the house, especially on my bathroom mirror. We need to be reminded of our power and the fact that we are in control of what consumes us. The amount of space occupied by the devil in your mind depends on the amount of and kind of thinking that you do. How often are you thinking negatively, saying it won't work out, blaming others, your parents, your upbringing, your financial situation, your spouse, the kids, your job, your boss, and ultimately yourself for being where you are right now? He can't control people who think positively. He can only control people who think the way he wants them to think.

So how are you thinking about your life? God controls love, faith, and optimism. All the goodness belongs to Him, and I find comfort in that knowledge. When you change your state of mind, you'll see how life changes for you. This wasn't easy for me and it took some time, but it's worth the time it took because during that time I was growing and learning to see the difference in results due to my thinking. But we live in a world where people want results right now, and because of that, they go back to believing the enemy in their minds. They think that when they try something once and fail, it's the end of the world, they're not good enough, no one likes them, or they're just not cut out for it. They allow a few noes and disappointments to send them back to their old way of thinking, which results in their old way of living. How sad it is that we won't stick up for ourselves and the changes we so desperately want for ourselves and our family.

The enemy loves when you believe you can't change. His weapon is poverty. I remember sitting at my job wondering why I was there and how I would ever get what I truly wanted if I stayed here. During those times the enemy said, "If you quit, you might get fired from your new position, you'll lose everything, the kids won't be provided for, hubby won't be able to do it alone. Do you know how long it's going to take you to start over and create some stability for yourself?" He was there reminding me every day of how hard life would be, but my desire was to have freedom, a freedom I could never have sitting at a desk for eight hours feeling unfulfilled. So I quit afraid. I did it scared, and I went through some really rough times, but I didn't quit. I couldn't quit. I wanted it too badly, and I had a family to win for.

The enemy is in everyone's mind, but how much space he has in those minds is up to that person doing the thinking. It's not easy to think positively when your circumstances prove otherwise, but you are built for this shit. You were born with a gift, and that gift is going to provide you the life you dream of, and those that try to keep you from it will witness it. You have to be willing to make that space in your mind for that truth and hold on for dear life. Every day your thoughts will improve, and you will get stronger. You are amazing, and there isn't anyone living on this planet who can't access the power to push through the pain, discomfort, and lies to stand in their power. Fear has no power over you when you operate in God's power. All the tricks of the enemy are to discourage you, but how long are you going to live discouraged? How long are you going to let fear stop you from breaking through to the you that you know you can be? You know you can do it. Maybe you're worried about letting others down, leaving them behind, disappointing your family and friends … but this is your life, not theirs. They don't get to tell you it's too late or that you're too old. They have no say.

God says it is time that you stop giving the enemy so much of your time and power, and give them to Him instead. You'll be amazed at how He works things out for your good. Some never see it because they never make the move that rewards them with that vision they so desperately say they want to see come to life.

The Enemy Is Always at Work, but So Is God

When you're discouraged, you're such easy prey for the enemy. He also uses other people such as your husband, neighbor, co-worker, friend, you know, those other people who are living in fear as well. They'll remind you of why you can't. I am sure they love you and want what's best for you, but how are you going to have the life you want if you're listening to someone who's been afraid to live their own? The devil has his agents everywhere, and they are always working. Some don't even know they work for him until they experience the light of God and come into a deep relationship with Him. I am speaking for myself too.

I was in my head for years about not being worthy or good enough, feeling like a failure for drinking so much, being broke, not being the best mom I could be, and not building my life the way I wanted it to be. I'm sure he loved that. Not only do you have to think about what you're thinking all day, but you have to love yourself through the process of making less time for negativity, fear, and doubt and more time for positive relationships and optimistic thinking.

When you feel poor, it discourages your independence of thought. It's almost as if you don't think for yourself anymore. You've got the power to reject those thoughts and make them what you want them to be. Don't let him corrupt your mind anymore.

He does it to us and to our children. He teaches them to drink and smoke, and cigarettes and liquor destroy the power of thought. These habits come in pairs and invite looseness into other areas of your life. The enemy gets to the kids through us and also through their environment. When we want better for ourselves and them, we have to look around and ask if better is around us. If you want *better*, you have to create it.

We can't act as if this life we live is a surprise to us because it's not. It's all a manifestation of what we have been thinking and saying. The lack of money, love, support—all of those thoughts have become things for you. Millions are victims of the enemy, and young girls and boys are learning by observing their parents. It's never too late, and it doesn't matter how old your children are. Freedom of thought exists right now. You have the freedom right now to stop listening to the news, picking up the phone for that negative friend, spending time in discouraging environments, continuing a habit that's destroying you and preventing you from growing. So many things will depress you if you let them.

The enemy is always at work, but so is God. Who are you going to allow to work through you? You have to get silent and stop giving everyone so much of your time. You need this time for you to get quiet and observe your thoughts. Don't be ignorant and think that this doesn't matter. The enemy loves dominating through fear and ignorance. I remember thinking, in my immaturity, that it didn't matter if I still hung with people who were doing the same shit in their lives, as long as I was not. That was far from the truth. I have so much love for so many people, but when I realized that being ignorant set me up to be dominated by the devil, I just couldn't bring that into my home, my marriage, my motherhood, and my business. Sometimes you just have to admit your decisions aren't always the best, and it's why you need time to think so that you're not living life reacting and saying yes to everything when you know you shouldn't.

Take Back Control

Don't Be a Drifter

A drifter is someone who accepts whatever life throws their way. A drifter doesn't know what they want and is too lazy to use their own mind. Ideas can be easily planted into a drifter's mind. Then they see themself living a life they're not happy with resulting from the thoughts in their mind. Don't let the enemy manipulate you anymore. You have everything it takes to break through this season in your life. You no longer have to bang your head against the wall, drink your life away, cry about the past, or blame others. You have to change the way you think by changing the way you look at life.

Your mind is nothing more than the sum of your habits. Your habitual way of thinking has gotten you to where you are now. We all have habits and routines. We do the same thing every day and don't realize when those habits are preventing us from living a life we feel so far from. You're not far at all. You don't need anything material from this world to change the things you think about. Are you always thinking that life is hard? Well, that's a habit, and you need to stop thinking like that. I felt stuck for a long time, and kept saying, "No matter how hard I try, I can't change." And, of course, that's just the way life was day after day. I refused to let the enemy have control of me. He gave me the weaknesses of my ancestors, and now that I know that, it's time to break some generational curses. You don't have to be like your mother, your grandmother, or even the you that you were yesterday. Think about what you're going to do to be different.

Most of us think going to school will make a difference. I am the first person to finish college in my family but, seriously, that gave me student loans up the ass and no real aim in life. Some of us through school without aim or purpose, and it's why we stay stuck or end up in a profession we're unhappy with. It's not what God told us to do. You've probably been nudged to jump off the deep end and start a business, but you were too afraid to, so you thought, "What can I do to move ahead in life without paying a big price?" We get desperate for change and make decisions like going back to school, but did you give it any serious thought? Did you envision what life would really look like after you completed college? Did you take into consideration the lifestyle your profession would give you, or were you only thinking about the money? Did you have a plan, or did you just think, "I'm going to go back to school because if I don't, I won't get the raise or promotion"? Maybe that raise wouldn't even change your life drastically, but you couldn't stand the thought of not doing anything at all with your life. But are you really just looking for a raise or a promotion, or are you looking for a life with meaning that makes you want to jump up and touch the sky in the morning? It happens all the time; we aim so low out of fear, that we end up with a life that's unfulfilling. We have to think outside the box in which we are now standing. I'm not trying to do what everyone else is doing. Are you? Am I wrong for being ambitious and thinking I can be somebody and make it without schooling? No. And neither are you. Teachers who are unfulfilled and going through their own hell are used by the enemy too. These teachers help the enemy by teaching you everything besides how to use your mind. I am not blaming them, but can you see how easy it is put yourself in environments that won't help you grow? Life is about looking within and not chasing a diploma or working for work's sake.

Damn it, I get so fired up inside when I think of the many ways in which we are told to live a better life, and none of them have anything to do with learning who you are and what you want your life to be like. In school, many of us adopt the thoughts of others and never learn to think for ourselves. Have you ever cheated on an exam, copied someone's project because you felt they knew more than you, or their work was better than yours, or because you were just being lazy? The devil loves working on your mind so that you continue to be lazy, fearing that working toward what you want will lead only to failure. The truth is, the other students weren't smarter than you. You just never learned how to tap into your creativity, or find what was special about you, or accept what was different about you and use it. You might have been criticized and judged in the past, and that hurt you. You probably never moved past that judgment, and you believed you weren't good enough. We can't compare ourselves to others or keep copying and pasting someone else's ideas, thoughts, and beliefs—we have to learn how to use our own. We can't believe the things that others say about us. People will judge you for having less as equally as they will judge you for having more. You can't be afraid to be you. You can't be afraid of your own desires. You are unique. God has designed you to stand out and teach others a thing or two. You no longer have to be insecure about yourself and what you have to offer just because it's different.

I know a few friends who could blow right past their department and run it, but they don't want to seem like know-it-alls, or they are afraid to be their co-workers' boss, or they simply don't want the responsibility. So they stay where they are, and they have the potential to do so much more, such as bring their creative ideas to the table and be the change-maker … but they're too afraid. Who do you think is running their mind and planting those seeds of fear? You got that right, the enemy. As long as you fear something, the devil will access your mind via that fear. He can't exist in a mind that thinks in faith and courage, a mind that has a definite purpose. He just can't exist. There's no room for him. When you recognize the power of your own mind, you cannot be controlled by him.

Take Control of Your Marriage

Marriage is another area in which people's minds are controlled. Married people fight over money and are always busy finding faults in one another. My marriage was that way, especially when the devil used alcohol to control my mind, which controlled my decisions—and I've made some very bad decisions. We argued over the money I spent and blamed each other for how we felt about one another and what our lives were becoming because of our weak mindsets. Alcohol caused me to spend, think negative thoughts, and act in a way that worked against building a life we deserved.

I was so unhappy with my life and constantly wondered why I couldn't get ahead, get my money right, grow my business, change, follow through with the things I started. The enemy loves when married people fight over money. They want better, but they just won't get off their asses to achieve it. They'll go days without speaking because of money, resenting each other's life decisions and parenting skills, which breaks the kids down emotionally, leaving them resentful of their parents. It's a big show, and the enemy loves to sit back and watch it get worse day after day. Couples think things can't get better. They never come together with a plan to get out of debt, raise the kids with more love and less judgment and fighting. How can things get better without communication and planning? It's literally hell on Earth in some marriages.

It's rare when you have two people in a marriage who don't fear poverty or death. Often, both or only one live in fear of money running out, bills not being paid, or not having enough to make do. This fear keeps people shut down and walking in a dead state. The fear of becoming more is too strong, so the couple blames each other for their own shortcomings until the fear of not having enough grows stronger in one of them and they decide to do something different, so they don't remain stuck pointing fingers at each other and getting nowhere.

Take Control of Your Livelihood

The enemy teaches people to settle for any job where they can't find purpose. This usually happens when they've lived beyond their means and now have to get a second or third job where they just work to pay for bills. Do you ever think about why you work where you work now? What is the purpose of you being there? What exactly do you do there, and for whom? How does it reward you with the life you want? Maybe you've thought about it after spending ten years there and realize there's got to be more than this. Maybe you're realizing it now because it's cost you your physical and mental health, or even your marriage.

We all get trapped into situations that we give no real thought to, and do it without having a clear intention. I remember sitting at my last nine-to-five job back in 2008 thinking, "I hate sitting here all day. I miss my kids, I want more money, I actually want to do something I love." Above all, I wanted to get out into the real world. I felt trapped answering phones, sitting in an office for eight hours day after day desperately waiting for Friday to come. Why did I take that job? I'll tell you why—because it paid better than my previous job, and the work was sweet. I answered phones, relayed messages, did paperwork—a no brainer—and after six months, I could handle the work without a problem. But I wasn't excited about the work, and that's where I spent my entire day. To then go home and be stressed, unfulfilled, and pour that energy out on my family, all because I was too afraid to do something about it—this couldn't be my life.

Fear will keep you where you are and spread those deep feelings of unfulfillment wherever you go. You can't hide it. We learn to cover it up around others and act like everything is ok, but behind closed doors we know it's a lie. We know we want more. You might confess to a friend or co-worker, but what good is that if you're sharing with someone who isn't helping themselves out of their own situation? Have you actually spoken to someone who can help you? Someone like yourself? When was the last time you sat with yourself in silence and challenged yourself to find the truth? I remember sitting with myself and crying inside and out, begging myself to do something and stop wasting my life because I was too afraid. The fear isn't just going to disappear, so how long are you going to sit around and wait? Of course, the enemy popped into my head and reminded me of all the things that would go wrong if I decided I wanted to be brave.

Break the Cycle of Fear and Procrastination

It takes making the move to actually realize that you can. So, what's your move? The fears growing in your mind and in your marriage are not going to take care of themselves. You are in control, and without you, nothing can change. This is when fear really gets you, and this time it puts you in a straitjacket. For how long, is all up to you. Fear shows up as procrastination. You have been putting off that thing you have wanted to do for years. When was the first time you thought about being happy, successful, free, or in love? I know it wasn't yesterday, last month, or even last year.

You were born with the desire to be happy, loved, and free. How much longer is it going to take you to stand up to the enemy and shut him down and stop believing you aren't good enough, and that poverty has no place in your life?

You can't think about it, and then forget about it. That's a vicious cycle you are allowing to take place in your own mind. Think and act. Not so easy, I know, but I'm encouraging you to not let fear stop you. Your deep self wants more for you. That voice has gotten really loud within you, but you keep turning your back on it. It's telling you the truth, but you're afraid of the truth. The truth is bold, courageous, and powerful. It says things like, "You're not happy here. Look elsewhere, hire a coach, stop drinking, stop smoking, stop hanging out, work out more, take better care of yourself." There are things you want to quit, but you're afraid to, and you're comfortable with all the things that keep your life the same. The enemy surely knows how to keep us living the same life year after year, even when we are depressed and sick of it. Why are you giving your power away to fear? As you fear, drift, and procrastinate, you're like putty in the devil's hand. He molds you silently over and over until you're a fixed being feeling limited. You've allowed this, and now it's time to take your power back and do something different.

Oh, and when you're wondering where God is in all this, He's right there waiting for you to acknowledge Him, to believe in Him, to trust him; fear and procrastination aren't signs of belief and trust. How many times have you trusted a man, a friend, or a parent, and they let you down? You were willing to trust without worrying if they were going to come through or not. Trusting is not something you say, it's something you do. When I quit my job, I had to trust that I was going to survive and not die, and that is exactly what happened. Doing something about the very thing that drove me crazy and kept me up all night was the first sign of trust, courage, and a willingness to take a risk. The help arrives from there. God sees you, my love, and there isn't anything you're dealing with that is going to surprise Him.

Poverty is a contagious disease, and you'll find it within drifters, so you have to quickly get out of places that are contaminating you. Because if you have this disease, you're going to spread it to your husband, your children, and everyone you come in contact with. Then you'll wonder why the people around you haven't changed, and it's because you haven't changed. You'll even wonder why you can't give your children the life they deserve. If you knew what you wanted and weren't afraid to go and get it, you wouldn't be in the devil's hands. He controls the weak and not the people who think for themselves.

You've got to master your fears, and they will master the devil and his plans. Take control of your own mind and let no one abuse it. You have the power to reject the words spoken to you. He will cause you to give up if you let him. We all fail when we try to be strong and stand in our power, but every failure brings with it an equivalent amount of success. It's only a temporary defeat. Think of failure as a steppingstone, and don't let it keep you from trying again. How many times did you have to go out on the road and drive to become a good driver? How many times did you cook that pot of rice to master it? How many times did you try to lose weight before you found the method that worked best for you? Don't forget about all the times you failed which eventually led to success. You have what it takes to overcome whatever you are going through right now. Don't shrink and hide in a corner, and don't believe that it's too late.

There are people who love you and want to protect you, and there are also people who don't want to see you succeed because they're afraid of losing you. They're afraid that feeling left alone in a life they can't deal with will force them to level up. Not everyone is ready to grow when you are, and that can't be an excuse as to why you don't get started on that burning desire you have inside. The enemy works on people closest to you. It's time to open your eyes and be a witness to this. Sometimes we wonder how someone so close to us can see us wanting better and not join us. They don't have God's power; they are the devil's puppet, doing exactly what he wants them to do to slow you down, strip you of your confidence, and leave you believing you are not good enough. Don't let him win.

I hope you realize that fear is everywhere. We have to control it where it does the most damage, and that's in our own minds. God-like people know how to convert failure into steppingstones that lead to greatness, and they will never scare you about your future. Be mindful of who's scaring you and who's encouraging you.

If there is anything I want you to take away from this chapter it is that *fear is the gateway to poverty.* It destroys the mind. It robs you of your dreams—those big, beautiful dreams you have of traveling the world, repairing your marriage, giving your children unlimited love and experiences to cherish for a lifetime. There is a solution to every problem and no need to blame anyone anymore.

A Devil's Woman versus a God-Fearing Woman

Let's look at the difference between a devil's woman, and a God-fearing woman. I like to think of them as the poisoned drifter and the engaged, encouraged woman. A poisoned woman lacks self-confidence. She doesn't believe in herself. Somewhere in her life, another poisoned soul told her she was fat, a bad mother, criticized her cooking, her career, judged her life in every way possible, and contaminated her mind. She has since then believed that she is not good enough, and nothing she does is ever good enough. That poisoned soul could have been her husband, mother, mother-in-law, brother, ex-boyfriend, teacher, coach, friend, or anyone else. We all have that person who judges us, spreads rumors about us, and always wants to change something about us. Not only does this cause her to lack self-confidence, but she has no imagination and lacks enthusiasm. She feels like a part of her has died. Tired of the cold and mean treatment, she becomes someone who she doesn't want to be but doesn't know how to change. It overwhelms her, and little by little, she hands over her power to words that were spoken by someone who obviously wasn't Godly. This poisoned woman becomes ill-tempered. She will make the same mistakes over and over, start things and never finish them, overeat, exercise too little, distract herself out of thinking, become narrow-minded, and expect from others and not from herself. Does this sound familiar?

What does a woman who's engaged and encouraged look like? She has plans. She is doing something that is definite (me quitting my job) with the help of others. She has big goals and little goals. She's radiant. Her tone of voice and the look in her eyes bring life to the room. She doesn't procrastinate, and she makes her own decisions. She's organized. She helps others and never blames others for her mistakes. She's a go-getter, and a giver. She is an inspiration to all that come into community and contact with her mind. She has a mind of her own, and she knows what she wants in life. She doesn't lack purpose, despite her past mistakes. She doesn't fear poverty because she knows she has the power to get and create wealth. Deuteronomy 8:18 says, "But you shall remember the Lord your God, for it is He who is giving you power to make wealth, that He may confirm His covenant which He swore to your fathers, as it is this day." She is unstoppable.

Love Yourself!

It's time to look within and face the deep. The devil can no longer control me because I have discovered my own mind and taken control of it. When I quit alcohol, he tried to shove it in my face as much as possible, but I stood strong, and I leaned on God for strength. I closed the door to the devil, and I encourage you to do the same. You owe yourself a new mind. You have the power to be different than you were a minute ago. You're allowed, you belong, you are loved. Love yourself as you work on changing your thoughts—thought by thought. Don't lose compassion for yourself. This is the start of a new beginning.

Chapter 6

The Power of Persistence

Give up quitting!

How to Develop Persistence

According to Napoleon Hill in *Think and Grow Rich*, to develop persistence you need the following four things:

- a definite purpose backed by a strong desire.

- a definite plan that you consistently act on.

- a mind closed off to negativity and discouraging influences; that includes family, friends, and anybody you know.

- a community; a relationship with one or more persons who will encourage you to follow through with your plan and your purpose.

(Adapted from Hill, Napoleon. 2007. *Think and Grow Rich*. New York, NY: Jeremy P Tarcher.)

This chapter will help you to examine your life in relation to these four rules to help you stop quitting. After you've read the rules, take a self-inventory and be honest with yourself. What would you love? What would make you happy? Do you have a plan? Are you taking action? Are you blocking out the bullshit that others feed you to make you not believe in yourself, or are you surrounding yourself with people who will encourage you to pursue powerfully? Go for it with these four steps, and never look back.

Persist in *Your* Purpose and Desires

Building a Business

The more I failed, the more I wanted it. It was hard. I cried, I felt scared, but I didn't want to quit. Every time I picked myself back up, I couldn't believe I was actually putting myself through it again, finding a new way, putting myself out there.

Have you heard that you shouldn't do the very thing your heart keeps asking you to do? People are always telling you what not to do. Are you going to keep listening to these people, or are you going to listen to the voice within?

Building a business has got to be one of the toughest things I have set out to do. I don't say this to discourage you, but only to share my truth. During the first couple of years, I uncovered much more about myself than I did about the actual ins and outs of business. I have been on an emotional roller coaster more times than I can count—feelings that I bottled up because it was embarrassing to admit how stressful it was. I had this feeling all along that I was meant for something more, but I just couldn't get my hands on it. I knew I wanted to be successful, but thinking about the sacrifices I had to make and the work I had to put in made my head hurt. I feared other people's opinions and didn't gather enough momentum because of the fear of judgment. It was so sad that I was worried about what people who weren't even taking the risk had to say. I realized I didn't know God then, so there was a lot of headspace for the enemy to plant fear in my mind, and I wasn't willing to forgive my past.

Nine-to-Five Is a Piece of Cake!

I remember thinking that working a nine-to-five job was a piece of cake: you have a set schedule; you know what the work is going to be like; others fill in when you are out; your pay doesn't change—you know what it will be weekly; you get weekends off and health insurance. It's no wonder most women don't break free, even though they want to. However, all that stability comes with a price. Some want the more rewarding life, but the price is too high to pay. From my perspective, staying at a nine-to-five meant losing my power, and I love this power. It allows me to create my own wealth, travel the world, meet new people, and build amazing relationships with women who need my services. I even get to be a role model for my kids in terms of what following your dreams looks like. When I think of working for someone else, that price is too high for me to pay. I never get to walk in my purpose, explore my gifts, and help the people I'm called to help. I don't get to control my income, my time, my travel, or where I want to relocate to.

Whatever your goal is in life, just know you have to trade your life for that goal, so it better be a damn good one. Are you still dreaming? I hope you are, because you are meant for so much more. Those dreams you have to provide for your family are real. They're possible, and while I won't say they're easy, I will say they're worth it.

Pay the Price

The price of entrepreneurship is failure. You are failing and falling. I look back now, and I laugh since I actually love the failing part, because I never fail backwards. I always fail forward, learning something new and growing in more ways than one. Persistence is a silent power, and it's why people become successful. They never lie down and quit. They keep putting themselves through the fire until they get one step closer to where they need to be. Truth is, sometimes you don't feel one step closer. Even when you make progress, you always feel a couple of steps away, but that's the ego and inner critic in you. It shows up a lot in business. You become this perfectionist, and that actually slows you down. My coach says, "It doesn't have to be perfect, Tye, it just has to be done." I love that because it's true. You get better as you take action, and nothing is set in stone. You can always make it better.

So many women want to quit their jobs, be their own boss, make more money, find their purpose, but they don't because their husband, mother, father, brother, uncle, friend, or cousin doesn't think it's a smart move. As a result, they never pursue their own God-given dreams. Nobody knows what's the best move for you. Nobody can tell you to go against what you feel in your heart because they have no idea what's in store for you, and neither do you. Learn to forgive the naysayers, love them anyway, but make your move. If you don't forgive them for trying to hold you back, embarrass you, or call you out, you'll end up resenting them. And if you don't make your move, you'll end up secretly blaming them for where you end up. We as women hold on to too much guilt and worry about what everybody else is going to think of us if we take the lead in our forties. Hey, Colonel Sanders of KFC fame was past middle age when he decided to pursue his dreams. Do the thing that scares you. Pay the price. The price may be hiring a coach while you work your nine-to-five so you can create a plan for yourself to walk away from building someone else's dream and starting to build your own.

Give Yourself Grace

Two things held me back in business—not having faith (leaving my mind open to the enemy) and not forgiving my past mistakes, which meant not showing myself grace on this journey. If you're thinking about starting a business, my best advice is to give yourself grace. You are doing something that requires a lot of courage, persistence, and support to keep going. When I was tired of feeling like I was starting over every few months, I caught myself going back to my old programming, wishing my parents had set a better life for me so I wasn't struggling to create what felt almost impossible. I told myself to stop the nonsense, ditch the old programming, and get back to doing what it took because I was meant for this. That self-talk has kept me going. Fast forward, and I thank God for my business because I am doing what I love and teaching other women how to build a life doing what they love.

Work Your Plan

You need a plan. In ten years where do you see yourself? Think about that and see what comes up for you. What do you feel when you try to answer that question? Is it fear? That's normal. Remember to give yourself grace. We are all afraid when it's time to step up. But you can't let another year go by wondering what your future is going to be like. You can't wish to win the lotto or depend on hubby to make more money. You've got to become the woman who takes charge of her life and says *no more*. Stop being the one living unfulfilled and wondering why. You are the reason you are where you are. I know it's scary, but not making a plan to pursue your dreams is even scarier. Sitting at a job in your fifties, neglecting your health, missing time with your family, and worst of all, never getting to witness your full potential is going to hurt more than the headaches I felt building my business. Peppermint oil, prayers, and a coach could fix that. But sitting and hating your own life because you were too afraid to do something about it? Nothing can fix that—not time, prayer, oils, or love. You living in your purpose is what is going to fulfill you and heal your aching heart—not a new haircut, not a new outfit, not a new friend. Nothing but your own will to persist will heal the pain you feel when you're alone in your thoughts. Cultivating the will to pursue is the action you can take now to feel worthy and whole.

We're so busy distracting ourselves trying to ignore the very thing tugging at our hearts. We think if we get a promotion or save more money things will get better, and we don't have to stay up late at night worrying anymore. This is you trying to settle, and hoping for an easier way out. We tend to believe that success is for everyone else besides ourselves. No one is more deserving than you, and no one can do what you do the way you do it. God has given you a gift and chosen you to walk in it. Not walking in it is costing you.

To start planning, you don't have to see the whole picture, just like you don't have to see the whole staircase when you take the first step. When you're driving, you can see only a few feet ahead of you and not the destination. We must give up the need to have control of everything. The power that makes things come full circle for you cannot be controlled. Think about all the situations that you tried to control. How would they have worked out if you were in charge from beginning to end?

I remember when I was searching for a home because I was desperate to move out of the Bronx. I took an offer in Yonkers, and we were supposed to meet the lawyer and sign some papers. God knew that I didn't really want to move there, but it was the best place we had seen. The next day, we got a call that the owner changed his mind and didn't want to sell anymore. I was so angry, but God was showing me that in my fear of not finding something better, I was pursuing the easy way and not what my heart really wanted.

After that fell through, I tried to control the situation by calling the agent back, telling her to speak to the seller, and wondering if the deal fell through because he wanted more money. Here I was fighting in my flesh for what God had not intended for me. Are you fighting to keep your job or a relationship that makes you unhappy, or fighting to cover up your real needs and only loving yourself superficially? Think about all the areas you've been trying to control, but control is not giving you the results you want and need.

I was tired of house hunting, but I kept pursuing because I know that no doesn't mean no; it means not right now or be willing to be guided in a different direction. Now here I am living in a beautiful home in upstate New York that offers me triple the quality of life I would have had if that deal had gone through. You can't necessarily control if your boss is going to give you a raise or how far you advance at work, but when you pursue your dreams and build the life you want, you can continue to evolve constantly and live the life you dream of. Don't do average things; do great things. Learn to trust your gut and take some risks. When things don't work out, believe that there is something better in store for you.

Push Through Negativity

Value yourself enough to bet on you. How do you know when you're ready to move on? When you don't feel the need to tell your old story of why things aren't working out. That's when I knew I was moving on. I stopped bad-mouthing my parents, my friends, my family, and my boss. I stopped saying, "I hate being here," and just created a plan to get out of the places I hated. I started looking at me and only me. How can Tyesha do better? How can she move on? What can *she* do differently?

I know it's easier when we have support, and support feels good, but what if you never get the support you need from your parents, community, workplace, or hubby? Will you hate them for it? Will you stay where you are now until someone gives you permission, until someone supports your decision? When we were young, we couldn't wait to grow up so we could make our own decisions. Now look at us still waiting to make them. We had an excuse when we were younger as to why we had to live the way we did and suffer the consequences of helplessness. But as adults, we get to decide how we are going to deal with our circumstances to improve our lives. Haven't you waited all your life to call the shots?

Don't fill your brain with garbage. So many people think they need someone to guide their lives because they have yet to organize their minds. Begin to detox now the things that make you believe you are not enough. I had to unfollow people on social media who made me feel that because I wasn't where I wanted to be, I was some kind of a disgrace. I just couldn't deal with seeing that, because making people doubt themselves is completely contrary to what my work or my heart is about. This power in us can be used in the wrong way or in the right way that is authentic to us. Unfollow people who make you feel that your life would be better if it were like theirs. Know that you don't need to be like anyone other than yourself. You don't need to compare, compete, or present yourself like anyone else does. Pursue more of you, not more of anyone else. I've had to take breaks from social media because I could feel pushy marketers and coaches poking at the pain of the very same people they wanted to collect money from. Break addiction and addictive thoughts and habits. Surrender to the power that's greater than you. Your world will be transformed. Try again and get stronger, try again and learn something new. Anybody who wants to create a better life has to disconnect to figure out what they want their life to look like and how they want to feel. Take an hour or thirty minutes to ponder this. For this to work, you have to surrender.

Surround Yourself with Encouragement

Don't worry about the *how* just yet. I still don't know the *how* of all the great things that have happened to me and all the doors that have opened for me. If you're worrying about something, you're not having faith. Worrying is like praying for things you don't want. I had to put it up to God and visualize my new reality. The life force that grows a tree is the same life force that's able to bless you with the future you want. Plant the seed and watch God. He's powerful. It's beyond our awareness, the things He can do in your life. It doesn't mean He's not working when a week later your life is the same. No one plants a seed and expects to see the fruit in a week. I am teaching my children these same principles about planting seeds and accessing the power to pursue the life they dream of, not the life society tells them they should live based on their education, race, demographics, and experience.

You have to take action. You have to want your dream more than your current life, and much more than your past. You've got to let go of what has not changed you in years. You have to be consistent in reprogramming your mind to believe that you belong, and that your dreams are yours for a reason. There are opportunities right in front of you. But it's hard to see them before we take the risk. Life can be great, but not when you can't see it. You can't see much looking at the mountain in front of you, but you sure can see a lot when you're at the top ready to jump. It's time to do something new in your life and business. Break your habits and create a new mind so you get new results. Don't make decisions based on what has happened to you in the past.

Don't give up on seeking someone who you align with to help bring out the best in you and support you so you can build your business, take better care of yourself, and live the life you desire—the life God chose for you to live. Listen to your heart, and follow someone who encourages you to believe in you and not in them.

Those who persist and haven't given up have a purpose. They know why they want what they want. You should too, and you should never apologize for it. If you know what you're doing and why you are doing it, you can create success and make better decisions. Don't spend time thinking, "What am I doing wrong?" Quitting destroys self-confidence, breaks down morale, dulls your imagination, and drives away purpose.

Chapter 7

The Power of Silence

You are alive and beautiful inside and out. Meditate and you will believe this.

Silence is Your Reward

Your silence is your reward. You owe it to yourself to know what's going on in the deep of you—just you and you—no one else, alone in your thoughts without judgment but with compassion and self-love. Facing the deep is such a great awakening. If you're wondering why you haven't experienced it yet, that great awakening is a reward for those who endure the silence. For how long, how often, or how consistently can you be in search of the God within you without distracting yourself with social media, news, gossiping, mindless work, and meaningless chatter?

Meditation is Medicine

Have you tried meditating? Yoga? Have you tried to do the things that involve silencing your mind and connecting you to the power that lives inside of you? If you haven't, I encourage you to start right away. It's no wonder we are all so hyperactive and our central nervous systems are wired and we can't even think straight. Do you really think that you don't have what it takes to rise above your circumstances? If that's you constantly doubting yourself and doubting God's beautiful wonders, it's time to sit silently and let your breath be the only thing you hear until it takes you deeper into a world full of love and abundance. Anything you can imagine having is there, and there's no lack at all.

If you are already starting to judge yourself, stop right now. You are not some outcast or bad person because you haven't made meditation a part of your daily life. You are just unaware of your truth. You are beautiful, and there is no reason to wrong yourself. There's no reward in beating yourself up. You have the power to go search YouTube for a ten-minute meditation and do it. Give yourself the time you need.

Meditation will lead to no more living in a haze, asking the same questions year after year: "Why me? What do I have to do to get it right?" Listen to me, God has a plan for your life, and it can't go wrong. All your steps have been ordered, all your opportunities and the people who are here to help you are lined up, along with the people who are here to distract you. When you tune in to your power and access the mind of God, you learn who is who, and you save yourself from the hell many of us have blindly walked into. It's ok, we can learn from it and make it the way it's supposed to be. You don't need to question God anymore. It's time to sit silently and question yourself. I didn't grow up learning any of this, obviously, with my past. My parents didn't either. Do you see now why we have to forgive them, have compassion for them, and show them grace? God has already given them grace, so who are we to not?

I was never a silent person or knew silence until I had my last drink of alcohol. I loved going to parties, hosting them, listening to loud music—when I hear the actual words now, I laugh, because I sang death and negativity over my life without even knowing. I loved dancing till the morning sun came up and being surrounded by company. All these things I still love to do, but there is such a difference in the energy, the lyrics, the environment, the times, and it feels so much better now, as if I am actually celebrating wholeness and not just out looking to get away from my present reality. I invited distraction into my life in a way that I do not do now. That all changed when I stopped drinking. I was a heavy drinker and went from dark liquor to white, to then wine. I notice that's how many people do it to believe they are making better choices than before. But the root of it all was still there, unchanged. I was burdened and suffering, waiting to be healed. I never saw the day coming when I would quit, but I am so thankful I did because I never thought so deeply about the meaning of my life until I was sober. I constantly hid from myself, in need of only enjoyment and not truth. Sobriety allowed me to focus on why I was here, and that required time alone with myself and my thoughts without distractions. Alcohol was my distraction, and that one habit led my life astray. What is your distraction? Is it spending money, shopping, overeating, going out, binging on tv, gossiping, controlling everyone else's life, including your husband's?

Three years ago, I had my last drink of alcohol, and thank God, because I was tired of getting hammered and waking up feeling like pure shit. Plus, it makes you fat—yes, the fat is inside of you sitting on your liver and kidneys, making you sick, slow, and lazy for days just to recover from one night. I don't want to be slowing down at my age. Plus, all the money gone for what? To put myself under? No thanks, I'm trying to get where I've been held back from for so long and focusing on exercising, eating healthier, and building my business. Drinking was ruining that.

I love who I am sober, and I had no idea how much my life was going to change. But here I am realizing and witnessing the power we have when we say no to the things we are afraid to live without or quit doing. What am I doing here, and what have I been doing with my life all this time? Pondering those questions was an awakening moment for me. I refused to leave that in someone else's hands. I had already spent half of my life being ruled by the world. It was time now to allow God to do that work within me. I wasn't sure what exactly to do about it: do I sit there in regret about the time I've wasted, or do I show myself some compassion and move forward? I chose the latter.

Meditating isn't as easy as it looks, so don't overwhelm yourself. Start out with five to ten minutes if you are a beginner, and be damn proud of yourself when you get through it. To sit still without paying attention to your phone and putting all distractions to the side isn't something half of the world can do. It's why anxiety, stress, impatience, confusion, doubt, and fear are at an all time high and will control your life if you allow them to. Take the time to slow down your life. Rushing and living on the surface get you nowhere fast, and when you arrive, you're unsatisfied and unfulfilled. People are constantly reacting to life and taking in so much information that is of no use to them and that stays in their minds because they opened themselves up to it. What are you opening your mind to? Give yourself the gift of opening yourself up to a new world—your inner world of healing and restoration.

My Meditation Journey

The Power of Affirmations

I had the hardest time trying to be still for years, and even after sobriety, my very first meditation session was hilarious. After two minutes, I was already opening my eyes to see how much time had gone by. I would fidget and get annoyed and be impatient. It was the funniest version of me trying to be a version of better me. Every day I would try again. I was determined to find out what sitting in silence was going to do for me because, honestly, I felt like it was pointless at times. I would rather have been doing something like watching a YouTube video, being on a zoom call, reading a book, or repeating affirmations. I love affirmations, and they work. Auto-suggestion, or self-suggestion, is one of the channels I've used to influence my mind. No thought, whether it is negative or positive, can enter our minds without the aid of auto-suggestion. When you have tapped into the belief that you are the person you affirm to be, your self-knowledge increases and your world begins to unfold all the truths that you have found and believe to be true. My affirmation routine changed when I began practicing meditation. Affirmations became my own, more personal, deep desires, and not just empty words I was repeating because someone else had told me that affirmations worked to deliver a certain result. I spent some time thinking of what I really wanted for myself, and it was peace, abundance, and love. I wrote my desires down in the present tense, and I read them out loud twice a day. By following this practice daily, I communicated to my mind what I wanted in a spirit of faith. I was tired of sitting around focusing on how I was going to get what I wanted, so instead, I committed to living and speaking as if everything I wanted was already here. I know that is hard, and it might seem crazy, but it helped me to believe. For things to change, you must believe they will change. Without belief, how can we live? Affirmations don't work when you don't mix emotion or feeling with your words, and honestly, my emotions and feelings were not healthy premeditation. When you don't feel good about yourself and your life, no matter how positive your affirmations are, they won't influence your mind if they are spoken without faith and belief. It's a practice I encourage you to not give up on.

Becoming the Witness and Not Just the Speaker

It's funny now because a few people have pointed out to me that I whisper when I talk. I alternate between a regular tone and a whisper throughout entire conversations. It cracks me up thinking of people's puzzled faces as they wonder why I do that. I sat in silence to meditate and asked myself about it because, honestly, I didn't realize I was doing it. The answer that came up for me was, "You are constantly listening to yourself now; you are the witness and not just the speaker." It's mind-blowing that you can grow to be that conscious, but you can. Start listening to the words coming out of your mouth, and ask yourself, "Am I speaking life or death? Am I viewing things from a negative or positive perspective?" And if you are committed to your silence, you will learn many things about yourself, for one, why you are here. That's my favorite one. I am here to fulfill a mission of leading people to stand in their power and experience what life is like from that place.

Banishing the Demons of Doubt from the Mind

Even though I changed my lifestyle, moved to a quieter environment, stopped drinking, and associating myself with unproductive activities so that I wouldn't have any instability, temptation, noise, chaos, and uncertainty, those demons of doubt still existed in my mind. You can't escape them. Your world is in your mind, and that's the part that blows my mind to this day. Your intention for life becomes more meaningful when you know and understand there is no escaping the thoughts in your head. No matter where you are, you and your mind are always one. It controls who you are and where you are in life, no matter what you achieve or how far you have come. How is the you inside of you doing? Is it doubtful, fearful, angry, discouraged, hurt, shamed, or guilty? Or is that you loving, peaceful, abundant, healthy, and joyful? You only need you, and you will always be within you, needing you and awaiting you. You can't buy love, peace, abundance, health, or joy. First, you have to become these in the mind. Your mind is what changes what's happening around you. Whatever you are going through today is from past thinking. Your life is a result of the thoughts and beliefs in your mind.

In silence, I got to hear many of my thoughts, and I hit massive roadblocks when I uncovered a huge limiting belief: I felt like an imposter, afraid, and like a fraud. There I was leading and guiding women on a journey to wholeness and power, but I too was struggling, and this was what my mind thought of me. The subconscious mind holds all the shit that was programmed into us from childhood and will leave you living in the past. Do not become discouraged. Ninety-five percent of your subconscious programming happens in the first seven years of your life. So think about the areas struggle with, and how they relate to your early programming. Your programming comes from the people around you, your community, the ideals that were instilled in you, and your experiences. I had to remember this was what my old mind thought of me, but I had to let it go for it to no longer be a belief of mine. Where would I be now if I had believed those thoughts, if I had not recognized them and not even known they ran on repeat in my mind?

You have got to fight the old you and rise above the noise, the lies, and the bullshit that has filled up your mind over the years. Things other people said about you and the way they made you feel are not your truth. You are someone really special in this world, and I'm sorry if someone has hurt you, said mean things to you, abused you, made you feel less than, and put you in situations that made your life a living hell to deal with. But that was then, and this is now. *You are alive and beautiful inside and out. Meditate, and you will come to believe this.* I started a practice called yoga Nidra, which is yoga sleep that helps to calm the nervous system and allows you to connect with your deeper self. It awakens the sleeping self. It has been the best kind of meditation I have ever done.

There was a time when I was focused solely on making money and having more than enough so I could live stress free, but meditating has allowed me to see that I don't need money to be happy, and I don't need anything material to feel purposeful in this world. I needed to let go of these beliefs to allow myself to see change. As Bob Marley sang, "Some people are so poor, all they have is money." I remember shopping to feel joy, stocking up on supplements to feel healthy, demanding love from a man. Silence gifted me the peace I had been searching for and the awareness that peace doesn't come from other people, money, or material things. It comes from within. It comes from making space within yourself. None of what you're seeking can be bought or given to you from outside of you.

The only reason my husband is who he is today is because of who I have become. I endured all the discomfort of me changing and the polarity that existed between us, and it's why I am here today. I didn't quit trying to find the power living inside of me. The power in you will make the impossible become possible for you. God is amazing, and His Word lives in you. You are love, and where there is love, lack does not exist. You can create love and abundance in your life. Will it be easy? No. Will you feel like your spouse is holding you back? Yes. Will you feel that your growth isn't their priority? Yes. Will you feel like your interests are not as mutual as they were before? Yes. But life will all unfold so beautifully for you, and you will be the one to influence the change. You will then be able to spread the love around, and you won't have to fight in your flesh to change what you don't like. You will be the one to pick yourself back up when all you want to do is throw your hands in the air and give up. You are the one.

Drowning Out the Noise

It's challenging to sit still and not speak, but it's the only way I was able to quiet the chatter, focus on my desires, and discipline myself to follow every negative thought with a positive one. Meditation has been a blessing to my life. I can't see how we can get through life without it. Not being able to meditate stemmed from all the instability, noise, drinking, fighting, and all the moving I have done in my life. You've probably either moved often, experienced divorce, had children, weren't able to have children, lost your home, or got relocated to a new one. So many things we experience leave us feeling unstable, and life becomes unstable as a result. But it doesn't have to remain that way. No matter what is going on in your life, your mind doesn't have to be all over the place. You can focus on what you want right where you are. There is a better way. You have the power to drown out the noise that's on repeat in your mind. You have the power to change the way you think.

It took me longer than a year, but the year was going to pass anyway, and I had no plans to divorce my husband, no plans to give my kids away, and no plans to live the same life anymore. My only plan was to get to the bottom of how to make my life better. How do I create a life worth living for myself and my family? Right now, I am able to write this book, and it's coming from within me. You have a story to share too. You have many things within you. You have everything you want in you, and that's the reason you get disappointed sometimes because you think about it morning and night. Your inner self is always speaking to you, and when you don't listen because of fear, judgment, shame, or anger, the results make you bitter. Get quiet and listen to your inner being.

Could you imagine having the best support system and internal guidance within yourself, but never listening to it? Man, that's a painful storm to be caught up in. That's like you heading out to a place you've never been to before and not having Google Maps or Waze, just trying to get there by guesswork and your own pride. You'd lose so much time doing that. I want you to listen to you because you know best. You may not feel that way if others have not forgiven you for some bad choices you made in the past and you begin to join them and continue not forgiving yourself. How much more of this can your soul take? It wasn't until I gave myself complete silence that I learned I am the one who stops me, the one who judges me, and the one who inspires me. You are one who allows. Allow yourself to change who you used to be.

Writing this book hasn't been easy for me because I have had to silence my mind in a way I never had to before. I had to increase my meditation from ten minutes to a full half-hour, and that drove me mad the first time. An hour is the longest I have ever meditated without saying a word, and I can't tell you how uncomfortable it was—I wanted to get up and do shit. Nothing was more important than this meditation, so I had to fight the urge to break the silence. I struggled with my own thoughts writing this book, but the more I do what I think I can't do, the easier it becomes to prove to myself wrong. Silence and I have a love-hate relationship because I want to share so much of my awakening. But at the same time, I have to remember that silence is my reward, and it's where I found peace. I am not always present on social media because I show up only when God has a message for you, but I know those messages come from deep within. It's important that I respect the practice of balance in my life as guided by God—retreating into silence when I need to and showing up to inspire others when led to. It's why in my coaching practice I encourage women to give more of themselves to themselves as we do the work together because it is the only way to break free from your old self. I love it, and I am grateful for it, but God knows it challenges me to face myself every time He takes me to a place I've never been before. I learned to accept me for me, and let go of guilt for wanting the peace I so rightfully deserve. I hope this book blesses you the way it has me.

After so many years, I finally understand that my silence is my reward. It's for me. It's mine—where I meet my thoughts, my pressures, my judgments, my desires, and my God who frees me from all that doesn't belong to me.

I've felt guilty for going solo, for detaching myself completely from titles, duties, and responsibilities that others thought were mine. But I know from building this relationship with God that my responsibility is to bring Him glory and to help you do the same. I hope that you will meditate and be consistent, even if it's ten minutes a day. Doing so will improve the way you feel about yourself, and that's the only thing holding you back. You've got to get to a place where you feel better about yourself. There is great love here for you, and I pray that you intend to live it by listening to it.

Chapter 8

The Power of Money

Your thoughts are things and powerful things at that when mixed with definite purpose, persistence and a burning desire for their translation into riches or other material objects.

Napoleon Hill

Why Am I Broke?

I sat at my desk with a cup of coffee, feeling great that I had made it out of the rat race and on this entrepreneurial journey. But sadly, I was broke. I had a nice body and was taking care of my health, but broke and living such an unbalanced life. Wishful thinking was all I had—wishing I could make more money so I would feel like I had an actual business and not a hobby. I started comparing myself with other women in these moments, wondering why they were killing it in their businesses, and I wasn't. How were they making so much money and I wasn't? So I started to question my path, and God would nudge me all the time, reminding me that the work I thought I had to do to break six figures wasn't it.

"So, what then?" I asked God. "I know I love encouraging women. Why am I not financially stable?"

The answer came back, "It's not your business, Tyesha. It's not who you think you are; it's who you don't believe yourself to be."

What? "Ok, God, I know you love me, but what are you saying?"

"You're hiding from your past mistakes, and I need you to face them and fix them. You're broke because you haven't rewritten your money story. You pray, you read my Word, but you aren't living by the principles to earn more money."

Being an entrepreneur doesn't mean you're making the best decisions. Remember, entrepreneur is a title like anything else. Being a lawyer or a doctor doesn't mean rich either. We all make mistakes that hurt us, and we don't bother to discipline ourselves to sit in the hardcore truth of them. I knew God wanted me to get my money right when the wealth videos started to pop up in my email, on YouTube, or in interviews I'd listen to. So the question, "Why am I broke?" was in my heart many times and was being answered through resources I didn't have to pay for. And the funny thing was that He placed the question in my heart to educate people on finances. You have no idea what that period of trying to figure out what He wanted and how He wanted me to go about it was like for me. I became really hungry to understand why I was broke and how I could rise above the poverty mindset.

Mastering Money

I asked, "God, why are you choosing me to teach the principles of money if my own money isn't straight?" He answered, "I am leading you, be still." All along the plan was for me to add this component in my training program because without financial literacy, houses will crumble, people will continue to overspend and put their families in debt, couples will continue to slave away at work until they are sick and tired and can no longer bear it, and kids will grow up to repeat their parents' mistakes. "Tyesha, pay very close attention to everything I am showing you, and sit silently so you know where you are to go next." I thought to myself, "This is not fun." A part of me was excited, but the other half was scared. "God, you really trust me with this?" I laughed out loud. "You have some sense of humor."

My husband has always been the one who was good with money and held it down, not me. But I trusted God, and the first thing I did was to get whole life insurance for $500 a month. "God, you are tripping. What about my car note, my car insurance, all my other bills?" The still, small voice kept asking me to trust It. I felt in my gut that I was doing the right thing, but my mind kept going from optimism to fear. I didn't know where this was going, but with God, you never know the next step until you are ready for it, and that's the beauty of living this life with His guidance. You never feel ready, but He knows what you want deep down inside, and if you listen, you will get it.

To make more money was always the goal. I wanted more money because, for me, more money meant life would be better. For God, more money in my life meant He could use me for the mission. We think things don't work out for us because the odds are stacked against us, but the truth is, we've lost our personal power. God is here is to restore and help you use it. He needs to use your physical body to do the work. I was disappointed in myself as a mother of two kids with visions and dreams of what I wanted life to be like, but where could I go without a plan? This question impacted my life, and it's why I ask you the same.

What do you want? What do you want life to pay you? It will pay whatever you ask. You have asking power, so use it. Don't be afraid to ask for more. You deserve to have everything you want, but do you really want it? You prove you really want it by doing the things that scare you. They scare you for a reason. On the other side are the life you want to live and the answer to end your struggles. What has God placed in your heart that you're afraid of doing? Pray about that because He is pursuing you for a reason. I was afraid to get my finances in order because I felt like I had no finances to begin with. It's these nudges that are leading you to the next step, but we don't trust them because of what our present situation looks like.

So I made the investments, and then I spent months reading the Bible and gaining interest in the markets. Everything I read for the next couple of months had to do with building wealth. The Spirit had literally taken over because these articles, videos, and podcasts would not have been my personal choice. I had no interest in any of this stuff. I just wanted more money; I didn't want to be a financial guru. The old programming was kicking in, of course, and trying to make me feel that there was no purpose in all this. But where there is a desire, you have to know it's there for a reason, and with me, the desire was strong. I am an early-nighter. Bedtime for me is 9 p.m., so if I stay up watching videos on investing and creating wealth until 2:00 a.m., that is God and not me. I could've said, "This is not me; this is crazy," but I trusted that this effort was taking me somewhere.

The plan was for me to get educated and see what I had been doing wrong all along and fix it for myself, for the generation that followed, and for the people whom I must help on their journey. We are all important to each other; we all need each other. It's always bigger than you and your needs. The very thing you struggle with is what you're blessed to help others overcome. You might question yourself and sit in your head feeling like you can't possibly do what God is calling you to do. Don't hesitate to make financial decisions because you worry about how you're going to survive. You were built for this challenge and, yes, you can do this. Within months, my finances were restored and He was providing for my needs, but the money that was coming in didn't burn a hole in my pocket like before. The urge to spend it wasn't there. I knew this was a time to trust myself with money, value it, do the right thing with it. I knew in my heart why He was sending it to me—to get all my bills in order, make more investments, and pay my taxes. He had a plan all along, and He was helping me to follow it. Every time more money came in, I took the time to ask Him, "What do you want me to do with it?"

What a beautiful way to see Him work through me. Might I mention that my husband was amazed and quite proud. Who was this new Tyesha … investing, organizing and growing accounts, allocating money, and sitting the kids down to teach them to pay themselves first? Take ten percent off the top and tithe, then pay yourself, set your future family up, fund your dreams, think of organizations or people you can bless, and start blessing them. It became a conversation I was no longer afraid to have because I was actually mastering my money and able to show my kids that I had a plan to do so. The conversation about money became more frequent, and I loved every minute of it. My old self didn't like talking about money because I had been so irresponsible with it, and I had nothing to show for it.

We can work our way out of poverty. We don't have to continue the struggle that our parents and grandparents lived with. We can put that struggling energy down and do something about the choices we make. I had to put certain things on hold, like shopping, eating out, overspending, and mismanaging my money until God finished showing me the bigger picture. We live in a world of instant gratification where everyone wants to spend money on material things and going out, which there is nothing wrong with, but when you're broke, in debt, and overworking because of it, that's when it becomes a problem. You are putting yourself and your family in a financial crisis, and you will pay for it. Don't resent God's discipline to restore you and bring you to a better place. Be forced to wait. You are not missing out if you are not where you want to be, and you're constantly praying about needing more money.

Take a look at what you've done with the money you do have. How have you been treating your money? How have you been thinking about money? Like it's never enough? Like it's hard to get? *You spend your money on what you value.* You have to check what you value and ask yourself if it values you in return. Is it adding value to your life or causing more pain, more debt, and more work on your behalf? You spend, overwork, catch up, and spend some more. What cycle are you in? Are you working for money or are you allowing money to work for you? Are you blaming money for your problems? Money is not in control of you, you are in control of money. How have you been using it?

I had to admit I was living above my means and not showing up fully in my business. To turn around and ask why I was broke was a joke. I had to become the observer to see that it was my fault. I valued alcohol, eating out, and fun times more than my family's financial freedom and more than the breakthrough my business needed—and that shit had to come to an end. Even if I had to start over, I was willing to do that, and I was willing to trust that God had my back through it all. You go broke on things that don't give you a return, so why not to build a new life? We are not bad people; we just made bad decisions. What it takes to get it right is still within us and has not gone anywhere. It's not too late for the plan your life needs to follow.

How Can Money Serve You?

Money means freedom from want. It helps you to live a more comfortable life, travel the world, and bless others. But often, our money goals are small, restricted to being able to provide us with food, clothing, and shelter. When you expand your thinking, be willing to admit that your choices need to change and actually do the work. When you begin to focus on what you can give and how you can serve the world, you will wonder where all this money has been all along. It will come in avalanches of abundance.

Our decisions come from our money beliefs, and those beliefs have to change. I constantly heard as a child that money was for the rich—*eso pa los Ricos*—whenever it came to a good school or opportunity. Eventually, I began to stop believing the things my family believed, and began believing that I was worthy of the opportunities, success, and the right to be rich. What a work to focus on, but life changing indeed. Your own family will tell you things like, "That's not worth it." I'll give you an example. When I was changing my eating habits and going meatless, I heard, "You're paying $7.00 for a loaf of bread, $6.00 for milk. You're crazy. That isn't worth it." I had to learn that other people's opinions come by the bunch, and they can mean something to you and change your mind if you let them; or you can believe that what you value requires your discipline. My health and my finances require my discipline, and I refuse to allow someone who doesn't share my values to lessen mine. Are you allowing that anywhere in your life? Are you allowing others to steer you away from your goals and desires because they don't think those goals are worth your time, energy, and investment? What those people think doesn't matter, but what you feel the need to do does.

It sucked to eat rice and beans for thirty days, not spend money, not go out, because living that simple lifestyle actually made me feel more broke. But I knew what I was planning for; I could see the bigger picture. You might be considered cheap when you do not want to spend your money on things that are too low on your priority list, but you don't want to part with your money for things that are not important to you. Whatever you value most is where you are most disciplined, reliable, focused, and organized. Everybody has a mission and a purpose in life, and it is always the highest on their list of values. I needed this discipline to enjoy life today without lying in bed awake at night worried about money, so I could have no strain in my marriage and say yes to the kids without going into a panic about spending money I didn't have.

What do you want? Do you know why you want it? What will it do for you and your family? What are you willing to do for it? You have to know what you want and why. Where do you want to live and why? What do you want to do for a living? Why? How much money do you want to earn? Will that be enough for the lifestyle you desire? Not being able to verbalize what I wanted in life inspired me to answer these questions and get to the bottom of my desires. I wanted to be clear about them. I learned that when we don't know what we want, we can easily be taken advantage of, lied to, misled, and that isn't cool. If you don't know what you want, then someone else will decide for you. What kind of life would that be if you had to do everything the way someone else wanted you to? It's time to be intentional and really answer these questions, no matter how uncomfortable answering them may feel.

Whatever we want comes with a price, and we have to be willing to pay that price for the things we say we want and the changes we want to see. If you tap into your desire and are willing to pay the price, you will begin to progress in life, and that achievement feels good.

Money is ready to come to you. It wants you to do the right thing with it so it can continue to serve you, not the other way round. But you can't keep shoving it away and then asking why it's not there. You are entitled to beauty, luxury, abundance. You were born to succeed and be rich. Wealth is a state of mind, and you have to organize your mind as wealthy people do.

How Do You Make Money?

Money is a symbol of exchange. That's all it is. So you want to exchange more. I had to start showing up fully in my business and pouring out my soul, coaching women like never before, creating a community for them, and setting the intention to help them get where they needed to be. It had to become about them and not me. Women began to appreciate my genuine enthusiasm and desire to help them boss up, create balance in their lives, and get their houses in order. It's why I make money.

Where do you get all your money from? You get all your money from other people. People use money. If you're broke, start being conscious about managing your money and provide a service. There is no such thing as something for nothing. You have to solve a problem, serve people. You have to find your truth and be courageous enough to put it out there. That idea you've been sitting on for years—do something with it. You are creative because you come from the creator. Focus your attention on other people, their needs, their wants. What service can you bring to this world that's important to others? Wake up and give. You might be thinking, "How can I give when I'm struggling?" Give some form of service to as many people as possible. You must give before you can get. I remember going out and giving a homeless man $20, and his gratitude made me feel so good. Just because you don't have a business does not mean you can't serve humanity.

There is money all around you. I receive it and pay God first, and the blessings continue. It's a beautiful cycle. *But we can't accomplish anything without a plan.* My old belief was that I had to work harder for more money, when, in fact, I had to boss up and stop doing the shit I was doing, carry out a definite plan, and not waver from it. Don't wait until a little problem becomes a bigger problem. Do something about it now. Get into communities that not only empower you, but that also educate you. I am never the smartest person in the room, and I love that. Take it a step further and hire a coach who is going to help you uncover your gifts and help you plan your way to success. Most of my money goes to coaching. I value coaching and what it has done to help me organize my ideas, be more strategic, and do things differently so I can continue growing.

My money follows my values and not meaningless nights out and material things. If I see something I want (like a new iPhone) just for the sake of having it or to keep up with the Jones's, I'll check in with my emotions and ask myself what this is going to do for me right now. Warren Buffet once said, "If you cannot control your emotions, you cannot control your money." I can't allow immediate gratification to cause me to give up before I can build the momentum to accomplish great things. I let the feeling pass and follow the plan.

I was broke because I couldn't put my pride to the side and face the root of the problem. I was broke because I couldn't say no to my guilty pleasures. I was broke because it was hard to break old habits. If you don't learn to program your mind for true abundance, you will stay right where you are now, repeating the same day, the same week, or the same year, over and over again. God is not withholding anything from you. Whatever you seek is available to you at this moment. You are always connected to His present-moment energy. God is power, and you have His power to create and hold on to wealth. Remember Deuteronomy 8:18 from chapter 5? "But you shall remember the Lord your God, for it is He who is giving you the power to make wealth, that He may confirm His covenant which He swore to your fathers, as it is this day." You can't lose with God living on the inside of you. When you face your fears, you will do the very thing that you are here to do, and you will be highly rewarded for it and be a blessing to those who need you. I believe in you.

Chapter 9

Embodying the Power That Is You

When I dare to be powerful, to use my strength in the service of my vision, then it becomes less and less important whether I am afraid.

Audre Lord

You Are Worthy

Do you ever wonder why you've done all the mindset work, all the spiritual work, cleaned up your environment, worked on your health, and you still feel like something is stopping you from being free? You studied the woman you wanted to become, followed her, read all the books, hired all the coaches, worked on your beliefs, and you're still struggling to believe that this could be you. Yup, I feel you. You still don't see the results you need to achieve your true empowerment and fulfillment. You have to walk in the shoes of the woman whose shoes you want to fill. You can't be half of her—you can't do only some of the things she does—you have to be her fully. Why have you struggled with embodying your future self? The one you imagine with the money, the nice house, the freedom to travel the world, the woman who is proud and admired by many, who can make boss moves and not feel like a fraud. How do we embody our power so we can see ourselves as truly deserving of wealth, joy, abundance, and freedom? Those deep negative beliefs that you have are hindering you. So you have to raise your deserving level. You have to look around and see what beliefs you are still holding on to. What story are you still telling yourself?

We say we want things, but are you secretly believing that you don't deserve them? Does it show because your life displays it? I couldn't step into my highest self because my feelings didn't match up with my thinking. I could think about being *her*—the woman I wanted to be—but I had a hidden belief that women wouldn't even see my worth, much less pay me. Again, why was I thinking that? Because I didn't feel worthy and see myself as the coach that I wanted to be or knew I could be. I had a fear of rejection. These beliefs were from past experiences I had to heal from. These beliefs are not true unless you believe them to be. You will *feel* the beliefs in your mind. Your thoughts are revealed in your emotions. Inside, I knew I could be great, but I couldn't freaking bring myself to feel it. Why? Because I didn't really believe it, even when I thought I did. Your feelings are the truth of what you really believe. I was afraid to step into *her*. Does that happen to you? You want to be this person, but you have a hidden belief that you don't have what it takes? You question whether or not you can meet the expectations of others. You think you'll fail or make a poor impression of yourself. I hit a wall when it came to embodying the woman I desired to be. It took a lot of God, coaching, yoga Nidra, and jumping off the cliff until

I could feel the truth about me. When you know your secrets, your fears, your bad decisions, and your failures, it is very hard to accept that you can change and be a totally different person. You hold onto who you used to be, how you used to do things, your past failures, what other people said or still say about you, and it feels almost impossible to rise above all the stuff. We're so accustomed to subordinating ourselves to outside influences that we never really get to know ourselves as the version that we are meant to be.

You Are Not an Imposter

Getting closer to Spirit and stepping into my power helped me to get rid of imposter syndrome. The list below, adapted from a T. Harv Eker training session, explains how to tell if you have imposter syndrome:

- You have difficulty accepting praise.
- You tend to discount your success.
- You're an over-worker to a fault.
- You feel a compulsion to be the best.
- You're often described as a perfectionist.
- The fear of failure can paralyze you.
- You sometimes avoid showing confidence.

Do any of these points sound familiar? These are the things that hold you back from embodying the version of yourself who is ready to live life abundantly. But nothing is impossible. Let not your heart be troubled, and fear not. We become what we think about. Have faith that you can be the person you dream of. Faith is the secret. What you believe to be true, regardless of anything outside of you, is what will be true.

Look Yourself in the Eye Every Day

Repetition is the mother skill of embodying the person you want to be. I stood—and still stand—in front of the mirror every day and talk to myself. I tell myself what a tremendous success I am: "Go out and be great!" Do you know how hard it was to look myself in the eyes and say I deserved success? But I never stopped standing in that mirror, looking at myself and believing that the me in this body, living in this time, is the woman who deserves to have everything she wants. That constant repetition of showing up and speaking life over myself began to change my feelings, so did showing up for coaching and hearing, "You are amazing, Tyesha. I hope you know that." It didn't stick at first, but eventually, it did.

Some women are inconsistent. They show up for a little while, don't feel great, then go into hiding again. They let their beliefs get the best of them instead of working on them until they create change. It's all about results. I want to keep working until I get what I want, and I want to be that *boss* version of me. I feel that now, I believe that now, I've branded it now, I'm unstoppable now, and there is no way I could do this alone. I couldn't embody the boss version of me without God, my coaches, my community, my daily practices, and consistency to follow through. Then one morning I woke up and said, "*I'm a freaking boss.* Look at the way I've turned my life around, and look at how many people I helped do the same."

I began to accept the truth and stopped holding on to the past version of me. When you feel discouraged because people don't believe in you, it's because you don't believe in yourself. You have to fully accept that you can be different right at this moment, independent of outside influences. You have to believe in yourself, and accept that you are a child of God, deserving of shedding the old self that no longer serves you. "Imagination is the beginning of creation. You imagine what you desire, and then you believe it to be true. Every dream could be realized by those self-disciplined enough to believe it." I love that Neville Goddard quote.

You can change your mind and choose to see things differently right now. You don't need money to do this. You've been programmed with the thought of "not enough" for so long, that you just keep repeating it in your mind and seeing it in your reality like a vicious cycle. But you are the only one who can break that cycle. The real magic happens when you stop waiting for permission. Stop waiting for others to be ok with your decisions. When you take action, doors will begin to open for you. Some people will not want to accept this new person you dream of becoming, and they don't have to. You have to. You don't need to show off anything new on Instagram or Facebook. The only thing you need is a new attitude. That's it!

When We Judge Others, We Judge Ourselves

Another thing I had to stop doing was judging people. If I wanted to be the best version of me, I had to stop criticizing other people's lives. I had to stop thinking some people were better than others because they were stuck in the past. Every time you judge someone, you are judging yourself. You hear every word coming out of your mouth, and it affects you. How do I look with a mouth full of scriptures but a heart full of hate? Unity of God Consciousness is seeing yourself connected to everyone. I had to make sure my entire life was aligned, and that took serious discipline. But the more you work on yourself, the better you feel, and the feeling of being a fraud disappears. You know in your heart that you are living right. It's hard to embody the next version of you when your heart is not right and when you don't feel like a good person.

God humbled me in this process of spiritual growth, and I know that I am to treat everyone equally, not judge a soul, and grow myself so I can help as many people as I can. I'm learning about the self-sabotaging role ego plays in our lives. Therefore, I don't live with an ego consciousness as much as I once did; I focus more on love. I know that the ego is not truth. Ego is the voice of fear; it tells you to hide; makes excuses; focuses on flaws; and craves the comfort of the familiar. It has separated me from myself and other people, made me feel like I was in competition, had me comparing myself to others, and feeling afraid when others reached success. I felt if others succeeded, then I couldn't succeed because their success robbed me of mine. My ego made me defensive and vulnerable to scarcity thinking. But now, I'm not self-absorbed, nor do I feel the need to validate what I have, what I do, or how others think of me—to myself or anyone else. Ego is slow, low energy, and separate from Spirit. Remember, the work is to be connected to Spirit, always seeing the good and being optimistic. Spirit can't win over ego if you keep telling it you are your old self. So allow Spirit to do its work in you, and don't fight it.

Four Habits for Success

According to T. Harv Eker, here are four things successful people do:

- They express their desires out loud, for example, *"I would love a raise."* This is the mirror work. Stand there expressing yourself out loud and having the courage to look yourself in the eyes saying what you would love to have.

- They are willing to ask. They have an awareness that they are connected to the source, so they know that if they ask, they shall receive.

- They state an intention, take responsibility for it, and won't entertain doubt; for example, *"I intend to manifest abundance and prosperity."* They have a knowing and don't need to prove it to anyone.
- They have a passion for what they want to attract. They use the negative and contrast to remind themselves that they're committed. Their solution comes from a burning desire.

First, you must know what you want and create an image that fulfills it. How badly do you want it? How badly do you want to be that person who loves their life and does all the things you imagine doing? You have to keep your mind on the image of your successful self, because we think in images. You have to see it for yourself the same way you see it for others. They are not more deserving than you. Their gifts are not greater. Keep your mind focused on your destination, and you cannot fail. Keep trying, and don't dwell on your problems. Focus on your solutions. Become a problem solver. Whenever something doesn't go your way, ask, "How can I make this better? How can I deal with this differently?" Entrepreneur and author Jim Rohn suggested, "To solve any problem, here are three questions to ask yourself: First, what could I do? Second, what could I read? And third, who could I ask?"

Jim Rohn also advised that you should work on yourself more than you do on any job or any business because it's you that matters. You can go from one business to the next or one shiny object to the next trying to figure out which one you fit in or which one will bring you success, but it's not the company or the product— it's you and your belief about what you deserve.

You only need the now, this moment you are living in right now, to change. Yesterday is gone, and tomorrow is not here.

Believe that what you are imagining is true. Trust God to save you. The silent power is always at work, living in your imagination, always breathing life into you, and ready to walk you through the action you're afraid to take. As you sow, so shall you reap. You must do the work and believe. Do the very thing that scares you, and trust that you are not alone. The promise is fulfilled through faith.

Blessings for Your Journey

I love you, and I pray that this book has blessed you with light and love. May the power in you be recognized and used by you. God is power!

About the Author

Tyesha is a phenomenal woman, wife, mother of two, entrepreneur, author and mindset coach. She empowers women to live healthy balanced lives, and helps them to find the strength and courage to persevere through life's difficulties. She has a no nonsense - no excuse attitude when it comes to health and using the power of your mind. She has dedicated her life to coaching women on how to "find their boss" and live the life they deserve, despite past mistakes. Tyesha's pain has given her purpose and she uses it to give back to the lives of others. Through her online platform, tyesharoman.com, Tyesha coaches women from a place of fear doubt and procrastination to standing in their personal power to live the boss life.

Join her community of bosses online at www.tyesharoman.com

With every donation, a voice will be given to the creativity that lies within the hearts of our children living with diverse challenges.

By making this difference, children that may not have been given the opportunity to have their Heart Heard will have the freedom to create beautiful works of art and musical creations.

Donate by visiting

HeartstobeHeard.com

We thank you.